How to
Age
Gracefully

T0413384

How to
Age
Gracefully

Essays About
the Art of Living

Barbara Hoffbeck Scoblic

SHE WRITES PRESS

Published 2025
Printed in the United States of America
ISBN: 979-8-89636-022-3
E-ISBN: 978-1-64742-881-5
Library of Congress Control Number: 2024926516

For information, address:
She Writes Press
1569 Solano Ave #546
Berkeley, CA 94707

Cover and interior design by Tabitha Lahr

Names and identifying characteristics have been changed to protect the privacy of certain individuals.

To my biological family, Peter, Laura, Theo, Steve, and Katee; to my Brightview Woodmont family; and to my editor, Britt Peterson, who took my words and turned them into a book, with love and appreciation.

Contents

PART 5: THE CREATIVITY OF OLD AGE | 103

PART 6: FRIENDS AND COMMUNITY | 139

PART 7: THE PRESENCE OF DEATH | 175

Introduction

In 2014, my husband of forty-six years died; in 2019 I had one terrible fall and then in 2022 I had another, breaking my back. After that, I left my longtime home in Manhattan to move into an assisted living facility in Bethesda, Maryland, in August 2022, when I was eighty-three. At the time, I knew all the stereotypes about assisted living: a place where people sit in rocking chairs, staring blankly into space. But the reality I found here was very different. In my assisted living facility, I've made friends, built community, and learned so much from the other residents and staff. I knew I'd tolerate living here, but I quickly grew to love it.

My experience has taught me that aging is more complicated than people who have not yet had the opportunity might think. As I learned sitting in the dining room, overhearing my fellow residents' conversations and taking notes on my cellphone, elderly people are not all the sweet white-haired old ladies you might believe. Pettiness, cliques, and rivalries are as rampant here as in any high school cafeteria, and people can be jerks. Meanwhile, however, the bonds of friendship and community sustain us, and as was true for me, many old people use the extra free time of retirement to develop creative practices that can keep them going even when things are difficult.

We are living in the undeniable presence of death. The ambulance visits regularly, and then everyone gossips in the dining room about who went, how they went, and who might be next. This constant reminder can be inspiring, terrifying, and sometimes mundane. After all, everyone, regardless of age, lives in the presence of death—old people are just more honest about it.

In this collection of essays and conversations, I've attempted to distill some of the lessons I've learned at my facility into something that might be useful for other people facing the later years of life. We are lucky to have made it here, after all, and we might as well use the time as best we can.

PART 1:

Adjusting to

a New Place

Just over a year ago, I moved to my facility, leaving Manhattan, where I had been for most of my adult life. The first night was horrible. I was so exhausted I couldn't fall asleep, and when I did I had terrible nightmares. In one, I was holding a rubber band, and from a distance I saw Earth. In the dream, I was thinking that if I could throw the rubber band hard enough, I could hook it to the North Pole, and then I'd be able to pull New York City back to me. So I did—I had the rubber band attached to the pole, I was pulling it toward me, then the rubber band snapped, and I was yelling, "No, no, I've lost my home, I've lost New York!"

In the other dream, I went back to my old neighborhood. I was walking around, seeing my building and the East River, then trying to walk to the Met. On the way, I went into the funeral home where my husband's funeral had been. The man who had helped me choose the coffin for my husband let me in and said, "It's awfully late."

I said, "I know it's late, but it's important, and I won't be there for long." He took me down to the room where I had chosen my husband's coffin.

He said, "I'll leave you here for a little while, but I'll leave the door unlocked." I went near the doorway and there was a funeral happening. But no one was looking at me, not even my two sons, and suddenly I realized I was a ghost. Finally, I woke up and it was light and I felt safe again.

The next night, I was so scared of the nightmares that I couldn't sleep again. When I finally got up the next morning, I was in very bad shape. I couldn't eat, but I sat in the dining room, and I started listening to people. And, that same week, I began to write.

Interrogation

You're new here.

> Yes. I moved in two days ago.

Where're you from?

> New York. Manhattan.

Did you work before
you came here?

> Yes. I'm a writer, and was
> writing when I had to stop
> in order to pack up.

Oh, that's not a real job.
Anybody can write!
What'd you write?

> Short stories. Memoirs.

Oh, that's fiction.
You can just make that up.

> No, not fiction.
> Reality. The truth.

Anybody can do that!
What else did you do?

Well, I'm an author—
a writer and an author.

Same thing!

No, as a reader, you do read right?

Of course I read!
What kind of an idiot
doesn't read?

Well, an author is a writer
who's been published.

Who's your publisher?

She Writes Press.

Never heard of it.

It's new. Founded by women for
women writers. Since 2019, when my
book was published, their booklist
has included several bestsellers.

Did anyone read your book?

Yes, I got several reviews.

Any good ones?

Minneapolis Star Tribune.

They're not serious writers.
All cookbooks and how to
raise grain and hogs.

How about Louise Erdrich?
She's a Minneapolis writer
and a Pulitzer Prize winner.

Any reviews out East?

I was reviewed by *Kirkus.*

That doesn't count.
You buy yourself into it.

Not true. You pay only if
you want to buy an ad.

Any important paper?
Wall Street Journal, say, *New York Times?*

Yes.

Well, which one?

The *Times Book Review* section.

A few lines buried inside?

Not exactly. Back page. One of
the week's top four, Not to Be Missed!
Excuse me, if you don't mind,
I'm going to sit over by the window.
By the way, tell me, did I pass?

Isolation

Shortly after I arrived at the facility, I came down with a severe attack of bronchitis. I was terribly sick: it was painful to eat or drink, and I couldn't talk well enough to be understood. My doctor prescribed powerful antibiotics, and I was kept in isolation in my apartment for three weeks.

My room is right next to the nurse's station, and I could hear the nurse reporting the statistics to the health agency. Bronchitis numbers were going up. COVID numbers were going down.

Aides and nurses didn't seem concerned about becoming infected, and they treated me much as they would any other resident.

At last I was able to return to the dining room. I sat alone as an extra measure of caution, lest I still be mildly contagious.

Right after I finished eating, the nurse caught me and took my temperature. Then she frowned.

I had to return to my room immediately. She grabbed my arm, pulled me into the elevator, and took me to my room. I didn't have time to say hello, or rather goodbye, to the new friends I'd barely met before my quarantine began.

In my room, the nurse administered a COVID test, which later came back positive, and told me I would have to stay put. "Now stay here," she said. "Don't go out."

The door slammed, and I heard the key to my apartment click into place.

It was the loneliest sound in the world. I thought of Sing Sing. Alcatraz. But my apartment did have a window, I reasoned. And the sky. More than food, the sky is essential to me.

With COVID, I was violently ill. At times I was so cold my teeth actually rattled. Other times I was so hot I threw off all the covers and asked that the thermostat be set at the lowest setting. Nurses began putting on their winter coats before they entered my room.

They also wore the shield mask that made it impossible for me to understand them. With my own mask on I couldn't use my nasal spray, and I was sneezing constantly. I began to have terrible headaches and bouts of gagging.

At one of these times, someone from the wait staff ran into my room. "Get up! Get dressed!" she said. She bent down to where my shoes and socks were, and held out one shoe. "Here, put this on."

I was vomiting, and I tried to indicate *Why?*

"You're missing your salon appointment! Here. Put this sock on!"

I could do nothing but cling to the side of the bed.

She ran to the door. "I don't have time now, but I'll be back, and you better be ready when I am!"

She returned in about fifteen minutes. I shook my head *No.* She shrugged her shoulders, and said, "Oh, whatever."

And closed the door.

After being quarantined for another ten days, I was becoming seriously depressed.

At a nonscheduled time, there was a knock on my door. I tried to say, "Come in!" but only a croaking sound came out.

There was another knock, and a head peeked around the door. I couldn't see who it was at first, but then one of my favorite waiters was standing over my bed.

"I know I shouldn't be here," he said through his mask, "but I just wanted to tell you that we all miss you and can't wait to have you back in the dining room."

"Thank you!" I said, as tears rolled down my cheeks.

Giving my shoulder a big squeeze, he said, "Hang in there! It won't be forever."

The next evening, I found a note tucked into the take-out bag containing my dinner. It read, "Get well soon!" and was signed individually by the dining room staff. Next to the names there were hearts. I put it beside my bed near my many tissue boxes, easy to see at night when the nurses turned the lights on in order to check my vitals and first thing in the morning when the sun moved around to my side of the building.

Another time someone hand-delivered a greeting card to my room. It was decorated with an antique map of the world, and it was signed by one of the activity directors: "I miss seeing you on the eighth floor," it read. "Hope to see you soon." I placed it on my desk where I'd see it first thing when I stood up—it inspired me to think about the travels I'd done and the places I still wish I could visit.

When I finally emerged, I was anxious to converse with my friends again. But the dining room was ghostly silent. Residents chose tables for two at the far ends of the room. After those tables filled up, people sat at larger tables but with their masks on looking down, or they asked for a takeout bag and returned to their apartments. If somebody sneezed, people at their table stood up and asked to be seated at another table far away.

In the spring, after vaccines became available, people started to relax. But then some relatives of residents contracted COVID, and after that, the dining room was silent and tense again.

Although all the staff and most of the residents, including me, did get the vaccine, residents didn't always understand how it worked. People were concerned they could still be carriers. It wasn't until two married epidemiologists living at our facility explained the details of the virus that people calmed down. Within a couple months of the vaccine coming out, there was a notable calm—but sneezing will still get you a nasty look.

My Village Square

After my quarantine ended, I began sitting on one of the entry benches outside my facility on warm evenings. There, I could see the world walk by.

There were the dogs and their walkers: mutts, pure-breds, a trio of Dalmatians, shaggy dogs and well-groomed dogs, even one large dog with a hind leg in a cast doing his best to keep up with the young kids in his family.

There were the children. Babies with their eyes peering out of their snugglies, toddlers testing the strength of leather harnesses. Three- and four-year-olds racing ahead to the street corner, testing the limits, while parents and nannies yelled "Stop!" Pairs and trios of preteens racing each other on foot, on skateboards, and on bikes.

And there were the two princesses. One evening I was startled to see two little girls, accompanied by their mother and grandmother, wearing beautiful saris, one sapphire blue and the other bright pink, both embroidered with gold thread. I smiled at them and said how beautiful they were. They stopped and thanked me. One little girl said, "How old are you? You look really old!" The mother and grandmother shushed her.

I said to the grandmother, "You have a wonderful family, do you mind if I ask how old you are?" She said she was in her fifties. The mother was in her early twenties. Then they asked, "How old are you?"

When I said, "Eighty-three," their mouths dropped open.

"Eighty-three! You're the oldest person we've ever met!"

In the meantime, the youngest little girl ran down the walk, unfurling her sari as she went and tripping, almost hitting her head on an iron railing. Her sister ran after her, grabbing her hand, and her mother said, "They are so different. One is very athletic and the other is all about being pretty and proper."

The second time they came by, they asked more questions about where I lived and told me that in their country, that would never happen—they'd be disgraced if they didn't have their mother and mother-in-law in the same house. She said, "We're modern because my mother has her own separate house."

The next time they came by, the mother said, "When I asked my oldest daughter what she wanted for her birthday, she said she wanted a princess cake and for you to come to her birthday party. I'll send you an invitation."

I thanked her. When the day arrived, I had a concierge here deliver my note of apology. Even though masks were going to be worn at the party, I still didn't feel comfortable taking the chance of contracting COVID. Later on, they sent me a photo of the cake—a doll stuck into a "skirt" made out of pink frosting.

Fractions

Two women at a dining room table.

WOMAN ONE, *to the waiter*: I'd like you to put my
portion of this pasta in a to-go box.
WAITER: All of it?
WOMAN ONE: Oh no! Not all of it, but not too much,
and not too little either.
WOMAN TWO: You know there's a reason we have
fractions! "Not half, but two-thirds, maybe?"

In the theater an hour later.

WOMAN TWO: The movie tonight is a wonderful one!
WOMAN THREE: But it's a very sad one, isn't it?
WOMAN TWO: Well parts of it are, but it has a
happy ending.
WOMAN THREE: What percentage of it is sad,
do you think?
WOMAN TWO: Oh, maybe 25 percent sad, 75 percent
happy. That's a quarter sad versus three-quarters happy.
WOMAN THREE: Okay. Well if you stay, I will also.
WOMAN TWO: Well, I'm definitely going to stay!
WOMAN THREE: Okay, I'll stay then.
She settles back into her seat.

Settling In

Two good friends of mine—one a new resident, the other an old friend who had often missed meals in the dining room because she'd been caring for her husband—individually told me that the other woman was standoffish: "She never says hello, doesn't even look at me."

It took me a few days before I could arrange for the three of us to sit together, but a wonderful conversation ensued: my new friend had been a renowned professional ballet dancer, the other reported on dance performances for major newspapers.

New residents sometimes struggle to connect to others. Sometimes that's because of emotional problems, sometimes because of physical problems. Beverly was a recent arrival. She had eye trouble and always sat with her back to the sun, wearing a safari hat pulled down to cover her forehead, a bandana to cover her cheeks and chin, a cloth mask, and long gloves. No part of her skin was exposed to sunlight. She seemed like a mannequin because she didn't turn her head and couldn't see. People thought she was rude because she never smiled or spoke to anyone.

But one day I talked to her. She was sitting near the back of the dining room, and I stopped by to introduce myself. As I drew near, I saw that she was crying.

"I'm sorry," she said. "I shouldn't be crying in public, but I just learned that I have brain cancer in the worst possible way, not by a nurse telling me in person or over the phone, but by receiving the news by listening to a voicemail! It told me of two appointments, one for radiation, one for chemotherapy."

"That's awful!" I said. "Did you have someone with you, or were you all alone?"

"I was alone, but my son, who lives in New York, is on his way here now."

I asked about her clothing. She told me she'd had a series of falls, and that after being hospitalized for one, she became acutely sensitive to the sun. She also had very serious eczema, and had to cover her arms so she wouldn't scratch them raw. We commiserated on many things: the falls, the eczema, the fact that both of us were lactose intolerant.

After that, I didn't see Beverly for several days. When I did, it was in the lobby, and I didn't recognize her because of her sun-protective garb. But her deep, clear voice was unmistakable. I asked how she was.

She had tears in her eyes.

"They're dying. They're all dying."

"Who?"

"My flowers. It's been a drought here for weeks! I always watered my flowers three times a day. Always in the shade because the sun will bleach the petals. I'm going to pray we get rain tonight so my flowers will live."

"I'm going to pray too."

The next day when I saw her, I said, "It rained last night!"

She said, "Thank you so much for your prayers."

I didn't see Beverly for two weeks. When I did, she was smiling.

"You seem to be much better," I told her.

"Oh, I am. A biopsy showed that I won't have to have brain surgery."

"That's great!"

"Any day that I can see the sun and the sky is a good day!" And, although she can't stand, she raised her arms up to the ceiling.

Equinox Cactus

Every six months, at the exact time of the equinox, my spiky zebra cactus produces overnight a tiny delicate white blossom on an impossibly long stem, and a pale yellow blossom with symmetrical lines of black radiating out from its center.

When I moved from Manhattan to Bethesda, the plant and pot were placed tightly in a cardboard box. The intention was to unpack it concurrently with my arrival.

That didn't happen. Eight months went by before it saw light.

I thought it had died. No blossom on the equinox, but a week or so later, the stem had grown as long as it had in New York, and on it, the tiny white flower.

Here at Brightview Woodmont, we have two or three spiky personalities. Pleasant and helpful one day, then belligerent and accusatory the next.

I wonder, were they deprived of emotional sunshine as children?

PART 2:

Adjusting to

a New Body

On the beautiful July Fourth weekend of 2019, I was crossing the street near my apartment in Manhattan, using a cane, on my way to meet a friend. I could hear the birds and there were flowers; I had just stopped and bought some groceries and a large pot of begonias, because mine had died. And then I heard someone yelling, "Stop, stop!" I looked up and a bicycle was speeding toward me. Rushing to get out of the way, I fell flat on my face. I thought I'd been blinded, but it was just the blood coming down over my eyes. I broke my arm and hand, dislocated my shoulder, gashed my head and back—requiring stitches in three different places—bruised my kneecap, twisted my ankle, and tore the ligaments in the arch of my foot. After months of physical therapy, I started using a walker.

Two years later, I had another bad fall, this time in my apartment, when I tripped over a power cord and fell on my side, breaking my back. Again, the recovery was immensely painful and very slow, and I moved into an assisted living facility.

I was always strong. I grew up on a farm; I traveled around the world. I miss my old body terribly. I miss walking—I'd so love to walk in a park alone again. I love walking with people, too, but I would love to be out there enjoying it in solitude. I miss the feeling of being cold outside, then coming in to the warmth—a very brief, pleasurable sensation. I miss showers. It's very hard when you realize it's never going to happen again. I remember asking my physical therapist once, "Will I ever be able to walk without the walker?" He said, "I'm sorry to tell you, but no. And don't try. You'll fall flat down."

I've had to learn to be humble. I see people in my facility who are stronger than me. They're told not to walk, and they try, and then fall and they end up in the hospital. I do not want to go to the hospital again. So I tell myself not to hurry. When I used to get around on my own, I'd be walking very slowly, and people would be very kind and patient. They'd say, "Take your time." One day I turned to someone who said that, and I said, "What choice do I have?"

I've also learned to speak up for myself in medical situations, to be a pest. You're handled by all these people: the nurses, nurse's aides, the runner to get you to the X-ray. I've learned to say, "I have a broken back, I just can't do that." I've learned to ask the nurse to count to three before he or she injects me with a needle: on one, I inhale and hold it, and then I don't feel the needle as much when it goes in.

And I've learned there are things I can still enjoy. Sitting outside in a park in the sun. The full moon. Eating a good meal. One of my great pleasures is sitting in the dining room and seeing the glorious sky at sunset. And music, music is so important. For Halloween this year, the facility brought in live music, a pianist and trombonist. We all watched and clapped. All the residents and their visitors were in one room together, laughing and stopping by to say hi or waving at each other. Enjoying the music together. It was like a bit of the old times.

Always Forgetting

One afternoon, about forty years ago, my husband, Joe, and I went to the Met, and then we turned back to go to this little coffee shop. Along that street were trellises of beautiful great white and lavender blossoms, and the aroma was magnificent.

Joe said, "You always remember the flowers, what's that beautiful flower?" It was wisteria, but I couldn't remember the name. And that was the first jolt that my memory might not always be with me.

Once it starts happening, it keeps happening. I work hard on names. In my facility, even the people who are in really good shape will say, "Oh, what's that person's name?" We are constantly reminding the people who are really bad—the ones with ten-second retention, who've forgotten the beginning of a sentence before it's finished—that it happens to all of us. Because one way or another, it does.

A new resident here is having severe mental problems, forgetting if it's time for lunch or dinner and what floor she lives on. And she's terribly frustrated that, now confined to a wheelchair, she has to wait for an aide to transport her.

"I always moved so quickly before," she'll say as explanation.

We assure her, all of us have been there. Getting used to our new, ailing bodies is one of the hardest parts of life here—none of us can fully accept that we're no longer young and strong and full of force.

Often a resident will say, "I'm forgetting more and more each day."

Which is true of the couple who sit near me in the dining room. From moment to moment, they can't remember what day it is, the name of residents.

One evening, the man can't remember his sister's name and his girlfriend supplies it. He's quiet for an unusually long time. "Are you okay?" the woman asks.

"No, not really."

"What's wrong?" she says.

"Maybe I have that disease. You know. The one where you can't remember things."

"Alzheimer's?"

"Yes, that's it. My uncle had it. Growing up, he was the father I didn't have, but at the end he didn't even know who I was. Do you think I have it? That terrible disease?"

"No, you don't have it."

"Oh, good."

I hear his seat cushion settle back into place as he relaxes.

Not to Be a Burden

This was during the COVID surge when no one knew how the disease was transmitted, hospitals and their staffs were overwhelmed, older people were dying alone, and the morgues closed down for weeks because there was no more room in their cold storage units.

My neighborhood, on the Upper East Side of Manhattan, was on the top of the contagion-zone lists. I went to stay with my son Steve and his wife, Katee, in upstate New York.

We did our best to follow the guidelines by not being close to each other. But I was unable to walk independently, so that was impossible. I felt terribly guilty! I could be the cause of one or both of them dying.

As the weeks went along and the cases in their district rose, I became depressed. Food no longer tasted good, and I had trouble sleeping.

One night I dreamt that I'd left the house with plans to walk into the woods. It was lovely out, with moonlight sparkling on the snow's surface. The steps leading out of the house and into the garage were covered with ice. I slipped and fell, injuring my right leg. Now every step I took was painful. When I stepped out into the night, a gust of wind hit me, and I staggered. I righted myself and struggled into the woods. The moon was full, and where there were a few trees, I found my way along the ridge easily. But when the growth became dense, I lost my way. I'd forgotten my scarf and gloves, and snow from the branches fell down my neck. Every part of me was freezing, especially my bare hands.

Nonetheless, I felt a compulsion to keep walking and made my way into the woods. The moonlight guided me along the ridge, but as I went farther, the moonlight disappeared. I fell and got up. Then, thinking of old, infirm Inuit women, I decided I had to go farther so my kin would know that I'd not been confused, but that my intent was to relieve them of another mouth to feed.

Then I fell down and couldn't get back up. But I'd changed my mind. I wanted to live!

"Help me!" I screamed.

I heard loud noises coming closer. Steve was at my side. "Mom, it was just a dream."

I was crying.

"Do you want to tell me about it?"

I shook my head. "It was terrible, too awful to tell."

"Your hands are freezing. Here, put them under the covers. I'll make you a cup of hot chocolate."

When I woke in the morning, the cup was on my nightstand. Untouched.

Around and Around

In the dining room, Sue Ann, dressed elegantly in a black-and-white checked Chanel summer jacket, rolls up to our table on her walker.

"May I join you?"

"Sorry, this table only seats four. The staff won't allow us to add another chair."

"Right on!" she says as she turns her walker around and rolls away. A few minutes later she's back.

"Can you make room for me?"

"No, sorry."

She shows no sign of any frustration or rancor.

My tablemates look back and forth at each other in mutual sympathy.

"We complain when we have to wait a little while for our food. We could learn from Sue Ann," I say.

All the while Sue Ann stands, leaning on her walker. Doesn't move.

"Try over there, by the window. Virginia is sitting alone at that table for two."

I instinctively point to the place, forgetting that Sue Ann can see only a few feet away.

After being prodded by a waitress, Sue Ann looks toward that general area, and then—taking the longest possible route—goes to the end of the dining room and circles around to Virginia's table.

I watch as Sue Ann and Virginia talk. Virginia shakes her head. Sue Ann begins to park her roller. Virginia shakes her head vehemently.

Obviously, Virginia is expecting a guest.

Sue Ann nods, and I lip read, "Right on!"

She heads toward the other end of the room where eight men sit discussing politics with vigor. She stands patiently until an arm thrown out in excitement hits her walker.

I hear one of the men say, "Sorry. No room."

At this point, I lose track of Sue Ann as I turn my attention to my dinner.

One of my companions asks, "Do you think Sue Ann has found a place?"

Looking around, I answer, "I don't see her."

The four of us are silent for a few moments.

"You know," I say, "Sue's wandering could be an analogy for our days here. Each day we circle from our apartment to the dining room, then to the activity room, then to our apartment and back to the dining room, on and on we circle until we retire for the night."

We remain silent as our plates are cleared.

As I leave the dining room, I pass Sue Ann sitting comfortably at a banquette enjoying a dish of strawberry ice cream.

"I'm glad you found a nice spot," I tell her. "Enjoy your evening!" I add.

"Right on!" she answers.

Too Many Movies?

L ast week I overdrew my Chase checking account. A minor matter, you say. Oh no! It took me more than twelve hours of my precious time over two days, trying to solve the problem by phone and computer. It turned out that the only way to access my checking account was to go to the Chase branch in person.

Jason, the facility's driver, picked me up midmorning and drove me the very short way there. When we entered the large glitzy place, I asked to speak to a manager and was directed to a window at the counter.

The first person I spoke with had a very quiet voice, and we struggled to understand each other. I asked if there was someone else I could speak with, someone who might understand me better. It was very hot, and I asked her if she could turn on the AC. No, it was broken, but she'd adjust the fan to cool me. But all that did was send papers skittering onto the floor.

After spending more than an hour, nothing had been accomplished except for my headache. It was finally determined, with the help of her boss, that the entire Chase system, nationwide, was down for the day.

In the car riding home, I had the strangest sensation: I'd been in that branch before. The decor, the glass cubicles, the large ugly art on the walls, it all seemed so familiar.

That feeling intensified as I got ready for bed. Was this an early sign of Alzheimer's?

I thought hard. Could I have been in this branch before? My daughter-in-law would've had to drive me, and I knew she had not.

Was I thinking of the branch in Manhattan? But no, that branch was very cramped and very loud, and everyone, both customers and staff, yelled at each other, and even then, they weren't understood. This one was made of acres of space.

Late that night, I began subtracting seven from one hundred. When I got stuck, I changed to repeating the times tables. Then I went to listing the presidents and the vice presidents. Those I did easily, but I got stuck at the secretary of state. Then "Blinken" came to mind, and I realized it was time for me to fall asleep.

Two days later Jason drove me back. I spoke to a different manager who was gracious and thoughtful. All went well, but there were still long periods of time when the two of us were waiting to be connected to the main office.

It gave me the opportunity to watch him and the others who were nearby. He and a tall, thin, very determined man who walked by—I'd seen them before!

Then I remembered. The whole set-up reminded me of *9 to 5*!

I asked Darrell—for that was his name—if he'd ever acted in a movie?

He looked at me quizzically. "No," he said.

"What about your relatives? A cousin perhaps?"

He shook his head, and I said, "What about the tall man over there? Has he been in any movies?"

Darrell said, "I don't think so. He's only been in the United States for six months."

He looked at me rather strangely, and I explained what I'd been thinking.

He commiserated and told me that a similar thing had happened to him.

Then, almost simultaneously, we said, "Perhaps you've been watching too many movies?"

The Art of Forgetting

Sometime during each meal, someone will say, "I wanted to ask you something, but now I can't remember what it is. This forgetting is so frustrating!"

Everyone commiserates. That happens to me all the time, the tablemates say.

A few days after my birthday, I received a package. I was pleasantly surprised. I hadn't been expecting anything. The box contained two gift-wrapped books, ones I hadn't heard of.

Obviously these books had been chosen with care. When I googled, I found they were perfect choices for me: books about woods and wilderness, about rivers and lakes.

When I told my friends at dinner that night, they said, "How wonderful! Who gave them to you?"

"I'm not sure, but I think it was my daughter-in-law," I said. "She always remembers my birthday. I'll email my thank-you tonight."

But the next morning, she emailed back, "It wasn't me!"

Then it must be my writing friend in New York, Vicky, I thought, she knows I like those topics. I texted her.

"No, it wasn't me! What are the titles? I'm always looking for a good read."

Then I emailed another friend. "Not me, but wish I had. What a thoughtful gift!"

For days I tried to think who could have given me the gift. Then it came to me! My niece-in-law, Beth. We often talk about books.

I emailed her, not expecting a quick answer. She and her husband, my nephew, are sailing the currents in the Gulf of Mexico. Days went by with no answer.

Then the other day my brother Bill called: "Is this my younger, most beautiful sister?"

He always starts our conversations that way, knowing full well that I'm his only sister. Our other sisters, Patt and Helen, are dead.

But he sounded frustrated this time.

"I'm still waiting for your thank-you," he said.

"For what?!"

"Didn't you receive a box with two books in it?" he said. "My daughter—your niece—chose those books and ordered them. And I paid her for them." (Bill is a firm believer in everyone paying his own way.)

I thanked Bill profusely.

He laughed as I told him about my long quest, and said, "Well, you have a nice list of people who might have done that, but remember I was the one who actually did!"

How We Face the Day

How are you today?

>Not better, not worse.
>And you?

Not so great.

>Oh, sorry.

I hate getting old
and falling apart.

>I know, but at least some days
>are better for you. Right?

That's true.

>Be grateful for that.

But that's really hard when
you're falling apart.

Less Than a Cow,
More than a Calf

Each resident here is weighed the first day of each month. May 1 was a disaster for me! The scale showed that I had gained almost eight pounds! The aide carried the scale in and placed it on the bathroom floor.

"Are you sure it weighs accurately?" I asked.

"Yes, but to convince you, I'll weigh myself," she said, and she stepped on. "Right on the dot! I weighed myself earlier this morning and got the same number."

I climbed on, and she read the number out loud. I asked her to recalibrate the scale. She did so, and when I climbed back on there was no change. I moaned.

She said, "That's a good number. It could have been two hundred."

In my early thirties, for a year or two, I began to worry about my increasing weight.

One year, when I entered my gynecologist's office for my semiannual visit, I was given a hospital gown and instructed to sit down and relax.

A scale was sitting next to the wall. I climbed on and toggled the weights on the beam scale back and forth, and then tried to read the number. I couldn't believe it!

I was back in the chair when the doctor came in.

"You look pale," he said. "Is everything all right?"

"Is that number correct?" I said, indicating the scale.

"Climb back on, and I'll check it."

The number was correct.

"Oh, my God! That's one of the weight categories my father used to measure his cows!"

The next day, I called my brother in North Dakota. He laughed.

"You don't weigh as much as a cow, but you do weigh as much as a good-sized calf!"

I'm Tired Of . . .

I'm tired of people telling me to stand up straight and of people telling me how to tie my shoes! And what shoes to buy because then I'd be able to walk faster and I'd be able to wear shorts and beautiful flowing pants.

I'm tired of people talking to me about the Harvard Business School hat.

"Why do you wear that old cap?!"

"Because it shields my eyes from the sun. My eyes are very sensitive to bright light. And it also reduces the chances of me developing skin cancer."

"Well, if you must, you should get a blue one. It'd bring out the blue of your eyes."

"But Harvard's colors are crimson, black, and white. And my son got his doctorate from Harvard."

"Well, that doesn't look very crimson to me. More like pink! You should buy a new one."

"No, I won't do that. This is the one my son gave me his first semester there. I'm sentimental about it."

"Where did you say he went to school?"

"Harvard."

"An Ivy League school?"

"Yes."

"Why, that's your problem, then! Nothing good ever came out of the Ivies!"

I'm tired of people telling me to move faster! I'm especially tired of people telling me how to use my rollator. I've been using it for five years now, and with physical therapy and a lot of practice, I've learned to do it efficiently.

It does require a lot of floor space. People order me to turn to my left. When I can't, they'll tell me, "You have to try. If you don't try, you'll never be able to do it!" But I can turn only to the right because the nerves in my lower back are dead, the result of a bad fall.

When I entered the movie theater the other night, a woman behind me said, in a schoolmarm manner, "Why don't you enter the row at the other end, it'd be easier for you."

"It'd be dangerous for me, especially so because of the steep slant. Knowing that I might fall down would make me very nervous, and with that, I would fall."

Just saying that made me unsteady.

"Well, you should start practicing *now* before you get any older."

A very tall heavy-set man, not seeing well, turned into my row and began to walk right on top of my feet and across my rollator. An impossibility.

I said, "Would you please go around and come in the other way?"

The woman who'd spoken earlier said, "Now she's ordering him around to make things easier for her!"

"I'm not ordering him. I'm asking him. He knows me, and he said he'd be glad to move down a row."

As I was getting into position to sit, the woman behind me said loudly, "You're blocking the view!"

The concierge dimmed the light. I leaned forward, my arm in the air as I struggled to find the opening to a jacket sleeve.

"Get your arm down!" the same woman shouted.

"Am I blocking your view?"

"No, but you're blocking someone's view."

I look, and there's nobody else back there.

The Theater Floods

All are in the Onyx theater on a rainy day,
watching the opening credits of Roma, in which a woman
sloshes water across a floor and begins to scrub.

WOMAN ONE: Is that the title of the movie?
  Only five letters?
WOMAN TWO: That's not five letters, that's four,
  count them, R O M A!
WOMAN ONE: Forget that. Look at all that water!
  We're going to be flooded out! Look at the screen!
WOMAN TWO: My gosh, that is a lot of water.
WOMAN ONE: I'm going to go up and get my galoshes.
WOMAN TWO: In America, we don't say *galoshes*.
  They're called boots.
WOMAN ONE: Well, I'm not American. I say *galoshes*.
WOMAN TWO: But you're in America now and we
  say *boots*.
WOMAN ONE: Come, come, let's hurry! We've got to
  get out of here!
WOMAN TWO: I'm not moving until you say *boots*.
WOMAN ONE: Berts?
WOMAN TWO: No, no! *Boots!* Try it again!
WOMAN ONE: Okay, I'm not good at pronunciation,
  I'm getting out of here and I'm going to get my

galoshes! *She hurries out the door, into a hallway that's just been washed and is still wet. She turns and comes back in.*

Oh my gosh, the water is this high, how much higher can it go?

WOMAN THREE: Well, what floor do you live on?

WOMAN ONE: I live on sixth, do you think that's high enough?

WOMAN THREE: Yes, I don't think it's ever gotten that high before.

WOMAN ONE, *leaving again*: I'm going to pray tonight that I get out of this alive.

WOMAN THREE, *straight-faced*: And I'll pray for you.

Call 911 or Not?

I had to wait a long time to receive my new coffeemaker. When it arrived, it was beautiful—sleek and efficient. And if it was filled with water, always reliable. But the other day in the afternoon, I was ready for a cup of coffee, and when I tried to use it, only a few little dark squirts came out and then stopped. I added more water and tried again. The same thing happened. I called for my aide.

She came in and said, "Why do you need help? That coffeemaker works."

"Well, it did this morning but it's not working now," I told her.

So she unplugged the machine and then plugged it back in.

"That should do it," she said. "I have to leave now."

I tried again. Again, the same result. I pushed the button for the aide to return.

Before she could come back, my cellphone rang. I took the call. A sweet voice was on the line, thanking me for my annual donation to the American Museum of Natural History. She started to explain that donations make a difference for educational programs.

While I was listening, I tried again with the coffeepot, pulling out the insert in the top of the machine. As I pulled, grounds came spitting out, hitting my chin, neck, and chest. She continued talking. "New York City only pays a very small percentage for education," she said. "Do you want to give a guess for how much?"

"I can't talk now, I'm badly burned!" I said. In an effort to avoid having the grounds hit me in the same place, I reached for the plug at a different angle, and hot grounds hit my finger.

"Ouch, damn!" I said. "That really hurt!"

With that, I gave up and went upstairs to get a cup of coffee there. But I forgot to hang up. Then I didn't look at my voicemails until I was seated at the dinner table. When I did, I heard a staticky voice saying, "What should we do? Should we call 911? She's badly hurt!"

Another voice said, "She'll be okay, it sounds like there's an aide nearby."

The first woman said, "No, we have to do something! We have to call 911!"

I left a message back: "Don't worry, I'm doing fine. Thank you for your concern."

A Wake-up Call

I was due to have a manicure the next day. On my right hand, I had a broken nail that I wasn't able to reach with my clippers. I was late arriving for lunch, so I didn't sit at my usual four-person table but rather at a table for two by the wall.

When I saw a friend entering the room, I began to wave to her. That fingernail caught on the edge of the placemat and broke off. It hit the dessert spoon with a *bing* that was followed quickly by a louder *bing* as it hit the soup spoon.

Heads turned toward me and everyone was talking at once:

What was that sound?
Is that all? I want to hear more of that tune.
When are you going to write the rest of that song?
I must remember not to sit with you!

As my friend sat down, she looked at me with a smile and said, "I saw where you were sitting. You didn't have to make such a racket."

Karen's Grand Return

Independent health aides come in a variety of physical sizes and helping styles, from the overly protective to the dangerously nonchalant.

Karen—at our table, we call her our sweet Karen—has an aide who hovers behind her, no farther than a feather away, sometimes keeping her hand on Karen's shoulder (as though she might fly away), constantly and consistently telling her to hurry and finish eating, then a minute later telling her to take her time.

Karen has a very expressive face and body. Without saying a word, she communicates her frustration. If we ask how her day is going, her tightly closed lips and a shrug of her shoulders say it all.

Her voice has always been very soft, à la Jackie Kennedy, causing listeners to lean in closely, in order to hear her.

Last evening, all of us had wished her a hurried good evening, when shortly later we saw that she was being hurried back.

The dining room manager intercepted Karen and asked whether she really wanted to return. Karen nodded her head vigorously yes.

Soon Karen was back at her place, the dirty dishes yet to be cleared away.

"Did you forget something?" we asked.

No. Then with great effort, she said, "There's something I must tell you."

She indicated to her aide to step back near the wall.

Then, with all the strength she could muster, she pushed herself higher up in the chair.

"I have an important announcement."

All of us sat quietly.

"I must tell you how important all of you are to me." She looked individually at each of us. "In this terrible time in my life, you've made it bearable."

And then, raising her arms high in a victory salute, she said, "And even made me laugh!"

And then motioning to her aide, "You can take me now."

As she drew a hand at the top of her neck, she was rolled away.

PART 3:

Adjusting to New People

Since I've been at my facility, I've had many chances to listen in to conversations. I didn't have to eavesdrop: voices carry easily in the large dining room and in the hallways. I take notes on my cellphone, often letting my meal get cold in order to capture the exact words. Then in the evening, I fine-tune them into the actual conversations that I overheard.

Just a few weeks after I came here, I began to publish the conversations in the facility's newsletter, and with that, people wanted to hear more!

"How did you do it?" they asked, when they read a new one. "That's exactly what I said."

I explained that as a child I wasn't included in conversations with my older siblings, and so I took to listening. Hearing what was not being said, the body language, as well as the words. Later, as a newspaper reporter, it was my job to take notes and report accurately.

These skills have been of tremendous use at my facility. Old people are often stereotyped in negative ways (as useless or slow) and in some positive ways as well (as sweet, wise, interested in knitting). The conversations I've observed here suggest that neither of those stereotypes are really true. The residents at my facility are tremendously accomplished people, but sometimes people can be rude or unkind. And often, clashes of personality can produce unintentionally hilarious results.

Men Discuss Literature

Two men at a side table.

So why did he marry her?

> Because she looked so good,
> especially from the back!

Who did she marry then?

> I can't think of who right now,
> but he was a great writer.

So you don't know everything,
do you? It was Arthur Miller.

> Just because I can't remember
> his name doesn't mean he
> wasn't a great writer.

Now there was another
writer about that time.

> Who?

Hemingway.

He wasn't a good writer!
He wrote for newspapers.

So what? Other good writers
wrote for newspapers also.
And he wrote books, too.

Tell me the name of
one book he wrote.

He wrote books about the sea.
The Old Man and the Sea.

That's set in Cuba. That means
he's not an American author!

What? A person can certainly
write about a place where he
doesn't live. He also wrote about Paris.

But he didn't speak proper French!

Well, an author can certainly write
about a place without knowing the
language. *To Have and Have Not*,
that's what I was thinking of.

You're just ignorant.

Just because I can't remember
something at the moment
doesn't mean I'm ignorant.

Do you know
about the witches?

Why are you talking
about witches now?

There was a book.
About American witches.
American witches are the
worst of all witches.

What are you talking about?
Europe had witches, too.
There was Joan of Arc.
She was a good person.

No. She was young and pretty
and pretended to be a soldier,
so she had to be a witch.

That's crazy. You're crazy!
I can't talk to you anymore!
Waiter! Waiter!
What's the cake tonight?

Leonard Bernstein

Two women sitting together.

WOMAN ONE: I was reading a review of a book about Leonard Bernstein this morning.

WOMAN TWO: Which paper?

WOMAN ONE: I read them all!

WOMAN TWO: You can't read them all. No one can read them all!

WOMAN ONE: What difference does it make? *The New York Times. The Washington Post.* I read every page of those each morning. They both had the review. The man died . . .

WOMAN TWO: That was a long time ago.

WOMAN ONE: Yes, I know that! Now they're recognizing his greatness. He was a genius, you know. A tremendous genius. *She raises her eyes to the ceiling.*

WOMAN TWO: He's not up there.

WOMAN ONE: Now you're being a smart one! When his father came into Lenny's—all his friends called him Lenny—bedroom and saw him in bed with another man, he was shocked. Wouldn't you be?

WOMAN TWO: I don't know. I don't have a son.

WOMAN ONE: Absolutely shocked. And he told Lenny that he was no longer part of the family. He banned him from the house.

WOMAN TWO: He banned Lenny's friend?

WOMAN ONE: No, no. He banned Lenny, his own son. His flesh and blood. Can you imagine? There's a Jewish word for it. Here I'm a Jew, and I can't think of the word. *She chuckles, looking across the table to a courtly man.* Now tell me, have you ever been interested in another man?

A long silence. Then courtly man replies.

COURTLY MAN: Do you mean romantically?

WOMAN ONE: Yes! I know you have a lot of men friends. You eat with them almost every night.

COURTLY MAN: Well, tell me: have you ever had a relationship with another woman?

WOMAN ONE: How dare you ask me that!!

COURTLY MAN: I'm turning the table on you! Have you?

WOMAN ONE: Well, of course not!! *Pause.* What's your answer?

Courtly man keeps her waiting. All are silent, waiting for the answer. After a minute or so . . .

COURTLY MAN: No. I never had a romantic relationship with a man.

WOMAN TWO: Now can we order some dessert?

Trivia Maelstrom

Location: Pub. Four tables near elevator.

RESIDENT ONE: It's five after two and nothing is
   happening! *Concierge passes by.*
CONCIERGE: Wait a few minutes, Claire's on her way.
RESIDENT ONE: How do you know that?
CONCIERGE: She called and told me.
RESIDENT ONE: Now it's eight after two! And I don't
   see Claire!
RESIDENT TWO: That's because she's not here! You're
   making me nervous, sit down and be quiet!
RESIDENT ONE: Where can I sit? Oh! May I sit here?
RESIDENT TWO: Well, if you must!

> *Elevator door opens and Claire,*
> *the facility's activity director, steps out:*

CLAIRE: Hello, everyone! I'm sorry I'm late!
VOICES IN THE ROOM: That's okay.
   That's *not* okay. The schedule says two, and it's
   now twelve after!
   That doesn't seem so bad.
   Mind your own business!
   Whew! We're in for a ride today.

CLAIRE: Let me put this bag in my office, and then
we'll begin. *She returns.* Who's ready to play Trivia?
Ready? The first question is, what's the name of
Elvis Presley's mansion?

Someone pulls out a cellphone.

CLAIRE: You can't Google for the answer.
VOICES IN THE ROOM: Why not?
    Because that's cheating! That's why! Give it to me!
    Grabs for it.
    I'll hit you if you don't give it back to me.
CLAIRE: Now, ladies. We're all here to have fun. Back
to question number one. What is the name of
Elvis's mansion in Mississippi?
    VOICES IN THE ROOM: That's too many *M*'s for me.
    What's that got to do with anything? Graceland.
    Stop saying the answers out loud!
    I thought it, and the word just came out.
CLAIRE: What season is it here when it's summer
in Australia?
VOICES IN THE ROOM: That's the third time you're
giving us that question! It's boring!
    But I wasn't here at the beginning!
    That's not my problem.
    Well, I had to go to the bathroom!
    Well, that's definitely not my problem!

Contest goes on ...

CLAIRE, *with enthusiasm*: Okay, it's time to determine the winners!

VOICES IN THE ROOM: Hurrah!

CLAIRE: Now we'll check the answers. *Claire checks the answers, then hands the winning table, table #1, chocolate bars.*

VOICE IN THE ROOM: That's not fair! They cheated!

Conversations in the Dining Room

Scene 1, Two women at a table.

WOMAN ONE: There! You did it again!

WOMAN TWO: Why? What did I do?

WOMAN ONE: You plopped your fat ass in my chair!

WOMAN TWO: Nobody owns a chair. If you want a particular one, come earlier. Then you'll have a choice.

WOMAN ONE: But I don't want to come earlier. This is my time slot!

WOMAN TWO: So now you're saying you own time! Ridiculous, just plain ridiculous!

*Scene 2, Waiter approaches
two women at table.*

WOMAN ONE: Where's my menu?

WAITER: It's right there in front of you.

WOMAN ONE: Oh. *Pointing to a line.* What does that say?

WAITER: Beef Stroganoff.

WOMAN ONE: But what is it?

WAITER: Just what it says.

WOMAN ONE: That sounds awful.

WAITER: Why don't you start with the soup?

WOMAN ONE: Okay. And bring me some tomato juice right away.

WAITER: Sorry, there's no tomato juice tonight. I'll bring you an apple instead.

WOMAN ONE: No! I hate apples!

WAITER: Iced tea, then?

WOMAN ONE: No! I hate tea!

WAITER: Water?

WOMAN ONE: Yeah. No ice. I hate ice.

Scene 3, Waiter approaches a four-person table and places his hand on a man's shoulder.

WAITER: Hello, Doctor! Here's your coffee just as you like it. And two hot rolls with butter!

DOCTOR: Now, don't think you can butter me up that easily!

WAITER: Ha, ha! That's a good one!

All laugh.

Scene 4, Two women at a table.

WOMAN ONE: Waiter, bring us menus.

WOMAN TWO: But you've already ordered.

WOMAN ONE: I don't think so. I don't remember ordering. If we all ordered, what did I order?

WOMAN TWO: I don't remember, but you did order.

Scene 5, Another table of two women.

WOMAN ONE: Where are the menus?

WOMAN TWO: When we get them, don't order the beef.

WOMAN ONE: Why?

WOMAN TWO: It's never any good.

WOMAN ONE: I had it yesterday, and I liked it.

WOMAN TWO: I'm telling you, don't order it tonight, it'll be dry.

Scene 6, Two men at a table.

MAN ONE: You're sitting in my seat!

MAN TWO: Nobody has their own chair!

MAN ONE: I've been sitting in that chair for more years than you can count. That is, if you *can* count.

MAN TWO: I'm a doctor! I can count in seven languages!

Scene 7, Two men at another table.

MAN ONE: In biblical times, it wasn't unusual for a man to have several wives.

MAN TWO: And how did that work?

MAN ONE: Very well for the men, I assume.

Scene 8, A distraught woman at a table by herself.

DISTRAUGHT WOMAN: Who took my straw? *She checks under all the napkins on the table. No straw.* How could it have gotten away without my seeing it?!

Scene 9, Young-looking woman stops at a two-man table to say good night. As the woman walks gracefully away, one man speaks.

MAN ONE: She's the nicest person here.
MAN TWO: I can't stand her!
MAN ONE: Why?
MAN TWO: She talks too much!

Scene 10, A waiter walking by a man eating at his table.

MAN: Now that is a *good* vegetable!
WAITER: All vegetables are good!
MAN: No. Some are better than others.

Scene 11, Two sweet women waiting for their entrees at their table.

SWEET WOMAN ONE: Why don't we all just kill him?

Sweet woman two: Well, that would solve the problem.

Sweet woman one: Yes, we'd be done with him. It wouldn't be that hard to get a gun. It wouldn't have to be a rifle, you know. A small pistol would do.

Both agree.

Scene 12, Barbara tries to sit down at a table.

Woman: Barbara! *The scream quiets the room.* Turn and look at me!

Barbara: Me?

Woman: You don't own that table! That's *our* table. Before you came, we always sat at that table. If you sit there again, I'll hit you. In fact, I'll chop your head off! *She extends her right index finger and draws it under her chin. Her friend starts chuckling and repeatedly mimics the motion. Barbara is in a state of shock and doesn't answer.* Barbara, watch your back!

The room is quiet for a moment, then . . .

Waiter: Anyone want ice cream?

Mean in the Theater

Saturday night in the movie theater,
watching An American in Paris.

WOMAN ONE: There's that strange woman!

WOMAN TWO: Where?

WOMAN ONE: Right in front of you!

WOMAN TWO: That's Barbara! She's normal.

WOMAN ONE: No, next to Barbara. She's weird, doesn't know what floor she's on, or if it's time for breakfast or dinner!

BARBARA: Do you know we can hear you?

WOMAN ONE: What? What did you say?

BARBARA: You can't hear what other people say, but they can hear!!

WOMAN TWO: She's not talking about you, Barbara, so why do you care?

BARBARA: Because she's talking about my friend. But you shouldn't say mean things ever! About anyone. *Turns to her friend and reaches out her hand.* I'm sorry.

FRIEND: That's okay. She does it all the time.

Shoes in

the Dining Room

A resident rolled into the dining room in her wheel-chair, hungry and ready to eat. She tried to sit at a round table for five.

"May I join you?" she asked.

"Sure," said another resident.

Dr. Steve said, "No, not until you put your shoes on!"

"What? I can't hear you."

Dr. Steve shouted it again, and the dining room director came over. "What's the problem here?"

Steve pointed to the woman resident's bare feet. The director said to her, "This is a respectable place. Would you go to a fine restaurant barefoot?"

"Why not?" she said. "I've done it before. Lots of times. But I have them with me. There're right behind me," and she pointed to the cushion supporting her back.

The director patted the cushion. "There's nothing there."

The director stepped away, but the resident was still sitting with her chair pulled up.

Dr. Steve said again, "You have to leave."

The resident replied, "I'm dressed for dinner. Look at you wearing shorts with your knobby knees hanging out. If I have to eat looking at your knobby knees, why do I have to wear shoes?"

"Because I don't walk on my knees!" he said.

"Well, maybe you should. Take you down to my size!"

The director returned with an aide, and they both began to wheel the resident away. As she was pushed out of the dining room, she looked back at Steve and shouted, "Well! I'm not going to invite you to my book party!"

Short and Sweet: Miscommunications at the Dinner Table

Scene 1, At two nearby tables.

WOMAN ONE, *upon overhearing WOMAN TWO speaking at another table*: Cockroaches?

WOMAN TWO: No. Chocolate mousse!

Scene 2, Another time, another table.

MAN ONE: You said King was an incredible student?

MAN TWO: No, I said my kid was an incredible student. Amazing! All straight As!

MAN ONE: Well, be sure to congratulate King for me!

Scene 3, Three women at a round table.

WOMAN ONE, *to female waiter*: What kind of dessert tonight?

WAITER: It's cake.

WOMAN ONE: What kind of cake?

WAITER: Jello. *Pronounces it* Yello.

WOMAN TWO: Oh, it's the white cake. Angel cake.

WAITER: No, it's jello.

WOMAN THREE: Jello?

WAITER, *getting frustrated and speaking louder*: It's jell—o!

WOMAN ONE: Oh, we're having Jell-O tonight?

WAITER: No!! It's jell—o!!

WOMAN ONE, *triumphant*: Oh, I've got it! The yellow cake!! The kind with the berry syrup on top.

WOMAN TWO, *smiling*: I'll have a piece of the jell-o cake.

All order the jell-o cake.

Scene 4, At the dinner table.

WOMAN ONE: I called, but it didn't go through. I bet she died.

WOMAN TWO: Well, she was 102! Or maybe 103!!

WOMAN ONE: At that age, what difference does a year make?

WOMAN TWO: Even at that age, a year does make a difference. You always want to reach your next birthday.

*Scene 5, Three women at a table
in the dining room.*

FIRST WOMAN: Wasn't that a great show yesterday?!

SECOND WOMAN: The movie downstairs in the theater?

FIRST WOMAN: No, no. The one we took the bus to.

SECOND WOMAN: I didn't go. What did you see?

FIRST WOMAN: Let me think. It was at the Reno, Reno, Renoir Museum.

THIRD WOMAN: Not the Renoir Museum. There's no Renoir Museum. Paintings, yes. But there's no Renoir Museum in the United States. There's one in France, but not in the States.

FIRST WOMAN: Oh, I know. It was another R word. The Rodin Museum.

THIRD WOMAN: You don't mean Rodin, you mean Renwick. There's a Renwick Museum in DC.

FIRST WOMAN: Yes! That's it! The Renwick. It had the most beautiful cloth coverings. Just beautiful.

THIRD WOMAN: What are you talking about?

FIRST WOMAN: You cover your bed with them.

THIRD WOMAN: They're called quilts.

FIRST WOMAN: Oh, yes, quilts. They were quilts. Did you go to the separate room where they had all the bright colors—red, blue—the most beautiful blue, just like the sea! If the people here were taking the bus, I'd climb on right now and go back to the Renoir Museum.

THIRD WOMAN, *in an I-give-up voice*: The Renwick.

PASSERBY, *to another resident*: Well, she may not remember the museum's name, but you sure have to admire her enthusiasm for art!

A Surprising Visitor

One night, I was suddenly awakened by my door opening and then closing. At first I thought it was perhaps a nurse coming to check on me. But there was not a sound. I said, "Who's there?"

It was still quiet. I kept repeating, "Is someone there? Are you in the bathroom?"

Finally, a faint female voice called from the bathroom, "No, I'm not in the bathroom. I'm in my room."

"No!" I shouted. "You're in my bathroom!"

She kept saying, no, no I'm not. At last, she came out, and I could see her in the bathroom nightlight. She was a small woman with white hair, and I thought she was my friend Davida. I said, "Davida! What are you doing here?"

No answer.

"Davida, I'm your friend Barbara. Talk to me!"

She started walking toward my bed. I realized she was my neighbor from across the hall, and I pushed the buzzer for the aide to come.

"I'm coming to visit you!" she said.

I said, "No! It's two thirty in the morning!"

She said, "It's not two thirty. It's lunchtime."

I said, "It's not lunchtime. And it's not dinner time. It's time for you to sleep."

At last, she opened the door to leave. I breathed a sigh of relief. But a few seconds later she opened it again and said, "I'm back!"

I said, "No, no, go back to your room."

She finally left a second time. I listened carefully, afraid that she was going to open the stairwell door. I was very relieved when I heard an aide talking to her in the hallway. Then he came into my room and said, "I'm very sorry this happened. I'll lock your door from the outside so it doesn't happen again."

I said, "Thank you very much," and I went back to sleep.

I usually get up before my English muffin and coffee are delivered, but that morning I slept right through. The very first thing I heard was a server calling, "I can't get in! Your door is locked!"

I called, "I'm coming, I'm coming," but of course she couldn't hear me.

Finally, I reached the door and opened it to let her in. She said, "The door was locked, it's never locked."

I said, "Yes, but a woman was in here last night, and it was locked so she couldn't come back."

The server said, "Oh, you had some confusion?"

And I agreed—there had been confusion.

Forever Out of Place

Sitting by my window around midnight, looking out into night and fog, I saw a shadow on the walkway below. Too late for dog walkers and for late-shift staff members, too. It seemed to be a very short person—but then the shadow suddenly doubled in size, and I realized it was a man, probably six feet tall, standing up from having tied a shoelace, perhaps.

With a slight limp, he moved down the walkway, which terminates in a grassy path, now in December no longer green, but stiff brown tufts. When he reached the grass, he turned right and walked a few paces, then turned right again, then again, finishing the rectangle. At every turn, he paused briefly and rocked forward over his toes a couple of times before gaining the momentum to move on. He made the same rectangle several times in a rigid pattern. The wind and the rain picked up. He untied his slicker from around his waist and put it on, struggling with the zipper for a moment and then giving up.

At one point, he stopped and reached into his jacket pocket for a loose cigarette and matches. He tried to light it several times with no success. Then he reached deep into his jeans pocket and pulled out a lighter. He flicked it a few times, but again, no luck. He ducked under a small awning by my building, where he finally lit the cigarette with the lighter—but only got a few puffs before the rain smothered it. He threw the butt down in the grass—then he bent down and searched for it, rain pouring down his back. When he finally found it, he tossed it into the fireproof bin at the back of the building.

He resumed walking his self-ordained grid. I saw him looking up away from the building, staring out into the dark as if he were searching for something unknown and mysterious. I left for a moment to brush my teeth, and when I returned, he was gone.

PART 4:

Looking Back

The sunset is tangerine and the evening air tastes like wild plum blossoms when memories of my mother are the strongest. Her presence is beside me as I relive moments from decades ago.

It was on such an evening recently when I looked and—there she was, walking into the dining room! As she grew nearer, my heart rate slowed. No, of course, not my mother, who I, and the world, had lost decades earlier.

The new resident's hair was a beautiful mass of black and white curls, just like my mother's. Her height was similar, and she walked the same—unhurriedly with a straight back, a slight curve below the neck.

She sat down slowly, placed her napkin in her lap deliberately, looked everyone who approached directly in the eyes with a slight smile, just like my mother had. Their hands were both beautiful with long tapered fingers, ideal for piano playing. Because of those fingers, each of them dipped ice cream from those small scooped dishes in the same way.

In my assisted living facility, we are all constantly reminded of our lives before we came here, going way back to childhood. For some people, those memories are fond: family, friends, a career that still gives us pride. For others, those memories can come with bitterness and regret: opportunities untaken, conflicts unresolved, the worry that one's life didn't really matter. Memories can be both a comfort—as I felt when I saw the resident who reminded me of my mother—and a misery. These are some of the memories that I've dwelled on most frequently here, as well as the memories of some friends and some overheard conversations about the passage of time.

Peonies

When winter at last had softened its grip, from the window of my childhood farmhouse in northeastern South Dakota, I could smell the beautiful peonies planted at the edge of our lawn alongside the rich soil where strawberry plants flourished. My mother had planted white and

light pink ones there several years after she was married. As a very young girl, I would watch her walk down to the peonies with a pan of cooking water from last night's dinner, then gently pull the leaves back and pour the water directly into the dirt so as not to waste a single drop.

When my older sister Patt was a freshman in college, she divided the plants that had grown bushy and added two dark pink ones that she'd bought with money she saved from the three jobs she worked during college.

When I was a young girl, in late May the aromas of the damp earth and the peonies would mingle with those of the lilacs and the apple trees. The opening of the peony, lilac, and apple blossoms coincided with graduation. We picked large bouquets of peonies and lilacs—the apple blooms were too fragile—and placed them in buckets to frame the stage of our high school auditorium. My siblings and I would each pass by them when it was our turn to graduate, holding our diplomas aloft.

In the last of those years, it was my turn to take that walk. My father, president of the school board, handed out the diplomas. As valedictorian, I was the first of my classmates to receive mine. The beautiful scent escorted me down the stage steps. After graduation, the girls would take the blossoms, snip them off, and use corsage pins to attach them to our dresses.

Many years later, long after my parents had moved from the farm, I didn't have the emotional stamina to go back. In fact, it no longer was our farm—other owners now lived there. One of my brothers did sometimes go back, and I asked him to describe the differences. When he told me how, in order to enlarge the lawn, the new owners had destroyed my mother's much-loved peony bushes, I was heartbroken.

Each spring before she died in 2021, my oldest sister Helen and I would report on our sightings of irises, crocuses, and columbines. Helen always commented on her blossoming peony bushes, describing the colors: white, pale pink and deep cerise. She also described her lilacs: purple and white, plus one tree that bore the blossom's namesake color, lilac.

That is, until her peony bushes grew so lush and thick that they became home to nests of voles. After years of trying to eliminate the pesky animals (every way short of poison), she grabbed a shovel, and after days of hard labor, dug the bushes up, and placed the rhizomes in a rusty children's wagon at the end of her drive with a "Free" sign.

During those same years, lilac roots were invading her house's foundation, allowing rainwater to leak into the basement. She managed to chop down and saw off the trunks and branches of the trees, but the roots proved a tougher adversary. After trying every tool she owned, she borrowed a plumber's pipe cutter to break through them.

I was stunned when she eliminated the peony bushes, devastated when she tore out the lilacs. But Helen balanced practicality with emotion, and humbly recognized that nature had won.

More recently, as a thank-you gift in April 2023, I ordered flowers for my daughter-in-law from an online florist by telephone. Due to language difficulties, the salesman and I struggled to understand each other for quite some time. My son and his family had moved since I had last sent flowers through this company, but the salesman needed his old address to look up the account.

The process was torturous. My son had previously lived on O Street. The salesman couldn't understand that there were no other letters to follow the O. And he kept adding the zip code numbers after O, rather than in the zip code bracket.

Then there was the unusual spelling of my son's last name. Why wasn't Scoblic followed by a K? the salesman repeatedly asked, because he knew a Hungarian family and their surname ended with K.

When I gave my address, he was thoroughly befuddled. The last time I had ordered flowers, I was living in New York. But now, my son and family and I all lived in Bethesda? Was I sure? he asked. And so it went on and on.

A day or so later I received a call from the receptionist downstairs, I had a bouquet. I called my son. They'd received one also. The photos we took showed matching arrangements of white roses with a few long stems of purple flowers, my daughter-in-law's favorite color, in a mass of green. I'd paid for only one, but when I called the florist, I was told there would be no additional charge.

I followed instructions: watered the bouquet regularly and placed the vase out of the sun. As the roses opened, their fragrance filled the room. As the days went on, I detected another scent, and when I pulled back the leaves, I noticed another small flower. A day later, as the bud opened, I could see that it was a peony!

For the next few nights, I went to bed with the two aromas intermingling, and with that came memories of breathing in the night air in my childhood farmhouse in South Dakota.

The Perfect Balance

*Dining room: A father sitting at a
table for two with his daughter.*

FATHER: I've lived a long life. I've worked hard and
I've played hard, and I have no regrets. I worked
day and night. Literally. I'd work hard for six hours,
take a nap for two, work another six, and so on.
Didn't matter where I was living. London, Florida,
California. I kept buying properties so I wouldn't
have to waste all that plane time. I owned three
residences in the States—a very large apartment
on Fifth Avenue, a large cottage in Greenwich,
Connecticut, and a smaller house in Manhattan,
in Greenwich Village. I was dapper. I had two
very large walk-in closets, one for work filled with
suits—dark gray and navy for the cool months,
beige and white for summer. I had specially made
drawers for my cashmere sweaters of every hue.
Now that's a word I haven't used in a very long
time. For play I had swimming suits—both boxer
type and the French bikini style in all sorts of
colors. For tennis I had the all-white regulation
shorts, some shorter to show off my legs.
His daughter laughs.

FATHER: Casual knit shirts, T-shirts they call them now. Long ones, and then the shorter ones as they became popular. Specially made drawers for my cashmere socks. I could go on, but I'm getting tired. But my point is all that stuff doesn't matter. I married twice and divorced twice. My true love is you. So beautiful and so smart.

DAUGHTER: You're making me blush.

FATHER: Don't hide it. You look tired today.

DAUGHTER: The plane ride took three times as long as it should have.

FATHER: And my two grandchildren. Handsome and beautiful and as smart as their mother, or they will be in a few years. I'd like to see them graduate and get on with their lives. I'm 102.

DAUGHTER: 103, Daddy. Remember we celebrated your birthday ten days ago?

FATHER: We did?

DAUGHTER: Yes—remember, your other grandchildren were there?

FATHER: My God! I forgot that I had other grandchildren! I'm losing my mind!

DAUGHTER: No. You're just getting old, Daddy.

FATHER: I'm happy. I'm ready to go. I've given you all of my money. You won't have to work so hard.

DAUGHTER: I love my job. I'll keep working.

FATHER: I'm ready to go.

DAUGHTER: Not this afternoon. Not tonight, Daddy! I treasure every hour, every minute that I spend with you.

FATHER: Promise me, you'll let me go. Promise me?

DAUGHTER: Yes, Daddy, I promise.

Your Shirt Matches

Many years ago, it was arranged for me to meet a young woman who my son Peter was dating.

The young woman was going to spend some time in India. I hoped I'd be able to give her advice from my travels there following my stint in the Peace Corps.

The young woman and I agreed to meet at an Indian restaurant in Midtown Manhattan. It was opulent, decorated with brass platters and samovars. I arrived first and was standing on the restaurant's beautiful burgundy-colored carpet.

When she arrived, before either of us had even said hello, I blurted out, "Look! Your sweater matches the carpet!"

When I told Peter about this, he hit his forehead, and said, "Oh, Mom! You didn't!"

As years went by this became a catchphrase, not only within our family, but also with my friends.

Sweaters matched eyes, earrings matched T-shirts, jackets matched sunsets, coats matched stormy skies.

One time my younger son, Steve, slid his Bronco off the side of a mud road. After great effort with me driving and him pushing, I looked at him as he slid behind the wheel and said, "Your blue shirt splashed with all that mud matches the sides of your truck!"

Now here in my independent living facility, beautiful white hair matches the crisp white of tablecloths and napkins.

The blue and purple of a black eye after a fall matches the tie-dye blotches on a T-shirt.

The bright pink braids of a waitress match the rich pink of a cashmere sweater.

And, of course, blouses match sunsets.

On February 14, I'd tossed on a T-shirt for an early physical therapy appointment. I kept it on for the day as I worked unpacking boxes that had just been delivered from storage.

I hurried to the dining room and was dismayed to see that it was adorned in Valentine's Day red: flowers, balloons, napkins, the works. And the residents were resplendent in shades of red.

My dear friend Vicky and her husband were doing a tour of Latin America, and we were corresponding by text. Wanting to relieve my angst a little, I texted her explaining the situation, with a photo of me sitting at the table.

Her reply? "Your yellow shirt matches the carpet!"

Last year, a few days after I'd broken my back, my doctor said I had to go to the hospital immediately. There the ER doctors gave me unimaginable news: I might not see another day.

My daughter-in-law sat with me until Peter could arrive. There wasn't room in the narrow space for three people and my bed, so my daughter-in-law stepped out and Peter, after asking the nurse if he could disconnect the beeping vital-signs machine, sidled his way around the equipment to my side.

What would I say to him in this moment, perhaps the last time we would see each other?

He smiled and leaned in close. I looked up and said, "Did you plan it? Your shirt matches my paper hospital gown."

End of an Era

Not long ago, my son Steve sent me a photo taken from the window in our Manhattan apartment. Looking out over a low nearby apartment building, the view is one of glittering skyscrapers.

That spot was the premiere place for taking photographs. Bright blue skies with a few puffy white ones, dark gray ones with a glimpse of blue poking out. Snowflakes drifting softly down or whirling in ever-changing patterns.

For many years we had great views of the Chrysler and Empire State buildings from that window.

I took photos of those lit up in appropriate colors: green on St. Patrick's Day; red, white, and blue on the Fourth; and a multitude of colors celebrating New York's winning teams.

Each year after September 11, 2001, I'd crunch myself into the corner in order to capture the narrow slice of sky with its phantom World Trade Towers beaming upward.

Then I'd press the photo button with tears running down my cheeks.

During holiday seasons, the window offered special moments. In one photo I caught the reflection of our tree joining up with two other trees in nearby apartments, a beautiful collage of sparkly lights against deep green boughs.

We were celebrating Christmas at my apartment that year. The weather was terrible with icy rain alternating with strong gusts of wind so the outside of the window was coated with frozen ice.

Theo, my ten-year-old grandson, sat next to the window. Our tree was at the other end of the couch.

I looked to the window and saw a reflection of our Christmas tree lights with Theo's profile superimposed on them.

"Look toward the window," I said.

He did so and laughed. As he waved to his twin in the window, I snapped the photo.

A Strange World

Five women at a round table.

ALL, *in turn*: It's a strange world.
   Yes, the climate's changing.
   A strange world. It's spring and it's so hot. In the eighties.
   It's August! That's not spring.
   Okay. But that doesn't change anything. It's still such
   a strange world.
   Maybe it's always been a strange world. Back through
   the ages. Way back. All the way back to the Netherlands.
   What? You must mean the Neanderthals.
   Anyway. A long time ago.
   Mmm, I'm going to have salmon.
   Again? You had it last night!
   I did? Well, I like salmon.
   Evidently.

Nothing Stays the Same

Is this the end of July?

> No, it's still June.

It's June 29. A long weekend! Almost,
anyway. I'd like to have my children
drive me to Atlantic City. We would
stay at one of the big hotels, walk on
the boardwalk, and gamble for a few
days. One time, on my first play, I
hit the slots, and the quarters came
tumbling down, making such a racket.
They piled onto the floor. People began
to try to grab them. I shoved them
away. That was a great night.

> You should've called for the guards
> to help you with all that money.

Are you kidding? Don't you know you
can never trust a guard? You can't trust
anyone! But I don't know if things are
the same. No, nothing is the same,
nothing stays the same.

Marianne's Monkey

Marianne asks us, "Did I ever tell you about the monkey?"

In unison, "No."

Marianne's story:

I grew up in a small town in Scotland. Is that a redundancy? Every town is small there. One night when I was about five, my father was very late coming home from work. He was a surgeon at a nearby hospital, a fifteen-minute bus ride away. It was a cold, rainy night. (Every night in Scotland fits that description.)

"You've never been this late!" my mother said.

"I know, but I didn't take the bus, I walked instead."

The bus company had strict rules: no chickens, hogs, pigeons, or any other animal was allowed. And my father would never disobey any rule. ("There'd be chaos in the operating room if everyone didn't follow the rules," he'd say.)

Then, with a flourish, he removed the white towel covering his lunch pail.

The long tail came first, then the small head.

"What is that?!" my mother squawked. (My mother never yelled. A refined Scottish woman didn't, and my mother was definitely refined.)

"It's a Rhesus monkey, the most intelligent simian," my father said. "If he lives with us, some of his intelligence may rub off on us."

"I don't care how intelligent he is! That monkey has to go!"

True to form, she didn't raise her voice.

The monkey went. My mother stayed.

Evelyn's Cherry Stones

When she was a young girl in Massachusetts, Evelyn's mother always walked her to school, rain or shine. The school never closed, so Evelyn and her mother were often wet and cold.

When making cherry pie, Evelyn's mother saved the stones in a kitchen drawer. Then, when the weather turned very cold, she heated the stones in the oven, wrapped them in old towels, and tucked them down deep in Evelyn's coat pockets.

In high school, Evelyn lived with an aunt in exchange for housekeeping. From there it was a fifteen-minute dash to school. This school closed when the weather was inclement, which was a relief to Evelyn.

Many years later, when Evelyn was weeding out her closets, she found one coat that was very heavy. There in a pocket was a packet of cherry stones. Still warm to the touch!

The Full Moon

I've seen the full moon in the most incredible places. Once with my husband, in Lichtenstein, we saw the full moon above a castle, shining on a river. Another time in Paris, we crossed a bridge over the canals, and a full moon was shining over the water. We walked along toward Notre Dame, and even though it was misty and raining, that made it beautiful, too. The bridge looked like a Monet painting.

I saw the full moon with my friend Georgia once, floating down the Nile in Egypt. The next night we asked for a river view from our hotel room, and when we went out on the balcony we saw the full moon over the top of the Great Pyramid. In Thailand, I saw an orange moon for the first time. To me it was just glorious—I didn't realize until later it was due to pollution. I've seen the full moon over Stonehenge. As a kid I skated with my eldest brother down the river as the light from a full moon guided us.

Once when I was a junior or senior in high school, I was having a sleepover with my friend Josie. I'd fallen asleep when she started shaking me: "Barbara, Barbara, get up!" I'm thinking, *Oh my God, what happened?* She says, "Come here, look out!" And there was a full moon shining on our little bit of land there. It was the most beautiful thing.

I see it here, early in the morning. And one evening as I was exiting the dining room I looked up and there was a double rainbow with a full moon hanging above it. It was so brief that by the time I went and told people, it was gone.

PART 5:

The Creativity

of Old Age

The first winter at my facility, bronchitis kept me apartment-bound for a week, then sly COVID retaliated, keeping me motionless for another two. During those lonely months, overwhelming boredom drowned my creativity. Silent, taunting Wordle and smug Spelling Bee destroyed my confidence, reminding me of what my mind once had been. I yearned for the clatter of dishes, the clash of walkers, the terrace view, my friends' good-morning smiles.

Looking out my window at the swirling leaves and the birds in the birdfeeder, I wrote poetry for my own sanity. The words kept me grounded; they connected me to myself, to a world beyond my room.

Since my husband died and I moved into this facility, I have so much time to write. I write only when I want to write, and I make my own deadlines. I don't have to worry about anyone else, about making dinner, about who's coming over.

Other women talk about it, too, the freedom. "I don't have to cook for a family of five anymore," says one of my friends. "No shopping!" They think it's strange how much time I spend writing. They say to me, you should relax, you should take time for yourself. But for me, it's fun. I couldn't bear not to.

Writing has always been like that for me. But here, I've tried some new things, too. One day I took a painting class. They gave us an option to paint a sky in purple and gray. I did it, and it was just beyond belief terrible. The teacher said, "Oh, if you rub it with something, that could fix it." But it looked like I'd dropped grapefruit juice on it. I tried again. This time, I worked very slowly and concentrated on the brush I was using and the color. I painted a branch and added a decal. And I was happy with what I did! I took a photo and sent it to my son, and he said, "Oh my gosh, it's lovely, save it for Katee and me!"

Never Enough Time

Dr. Bob, after working head down at the far end of the first-floor coffee lounge for more than an hour, gets up and passes by me, doing the same at a table near the door.

"There'll never be enough hours in a day, for good writers like the two of us," he says with a smile, "to write some more of our important books."

He gives a thumbs-up and continues toward the elevator.

The Time

I Tried Knitting

I never knitted before, but here they do a class once a week. One week, I went. The teacher told me to sit, then gave me two long needles and a roll of yarn. She did the first few rows, then she had to go help other students.

I had watched what she did, and I said, "Okay, I think I can do it."

I started, and right away I had trouble. Finally the teacher came back.

She said, "Okay, pull out the needles, now you have your scarf!" But it was a horrible mess! "Don't worry, don't worry, you can always try it again."

A couple of days later, the teacher came to visit me. I had stuffed the mess into a plastic shopping bag. I pulled it out and said, "Can you help me fix it?"

She laughed and said, "Barbara, you have to take it all apart and start over." I'll never try again.

Last year, they taught us all how to make pomanders. The teacher held out an orange and a clove. He said, you put the clove in the orange, and he showed us how. First, I tried a smiley face, but it didn't work. Then I made the smile go upside down, and I added wrinkles. It was a frowny face—it was my Bah Humbug pomander.

But other people here do beautiful things. At the holidays, they knit spangled scarfs that glitter, white and silver and red and black. They make jewelry with ceramic clay. They arrange flowers, make wreaths, and paint Christmas ornaments. When each item is finished, the director will say, "Beau-tee-ful, just beau-tee-ful!"

Mother's Perfect

Canned Pears

The National Service Women's Land Army poster on
my wall shows a woman guiding a dirt plow with her
right hand, sowing seeds with her left, and a baby in a soft
sling on her back being lulled by the rhythmic movement
of her body.

The farm women in our small community did the
same, although none of them had the slicker and hat that
kept the sun and rain at bay.

My mother couldn't be in the fields because she had
to stay near the house where my disabled oldest sister,
Dorothy, was crib-bound.

When I visited my good friend, Mary Lee, who lived
a mile away, she was proud of the number of hours her
mother worked each day. Though she still couldn't add, she

knew the shapes of the numbers enough to know when her mother had worked "five, not four."

When I returned home after lunch, I asked my mother for some dessert. Mary Lee's mother had served canned pears for dessert at lunch.

"One dessert is enough," she told me.

"I didn't eat it."

"Why not?"

"It looked rotten so I gave mine to Mary Lee."

After a little questioning she explained to me that what I thought was rotten was just a bit of peel clinging to a piece of the pear.

Mother always carefully washed and dried each piece of fruit before she peeled them, and then she peeled them so carefully that the fruit wasn't nicked and no piece of the peel remained.

She couldn't control much, but she could control the absence of a bit of a peel in her canned pears.

Our Mothers' Bread

This was after World War II when the food supply was short.

When I entered fourth grade, I was entrusted with collecting lunch money from students who weren't eligible for the government's food assistance program. I stood at the entry of the combined fifth- and sixth-grade classroom with an ink pad and stamp, and a small metal lockbox. When a student entered who didn't qualify, I'd stamp the small card with the day's date. The fee was ten cents, but because dimes were hard to come by (copper metal was expensive after the war), I usually was given two nickels.

I'd put the card in the box, and before I'd sit down to eat, I'd quickly multiply the number of nickels by the number of students. Then I'd add another nickel, payment for my "labor." My lunch consisted of sandwiches made with my mother's homemade bread and government-issued cheese or peanut butter. The bread was still warm when my sister Helen packed my metal lunchbox each morning.

When I opened the lunchbox, releasing the bread's aroma, my classmates would look at me enviously. One day, an upper-school student who'd just walked in said, "I'll trade you my sandwich for yours, and give you a nickel."

It was an honor just to be addressed by her, as she was not only much older than me, but the prettiest girl in the entire school. When I tasted her sandwich, made with store-bought bread, I loved the taste and the fact that it was much easier to eat. My buck teeth made it hard to chew crusts.

When I got home, I told my mother that. She didn't say anything, only nodded her head. After that, sometimes my siblings and I had commercial bread, but when we didn't, I'd come home with two nickels.

All this came to mind this morning when I read a recent blog entry posted by Father Eric Hollas, acting director of St. John's University in Collegeville, Minnesota.

He wrote that he'd grown up eating and enjoying his grandmother's bread. She lived on a farm with ample room for growing fresh fruit and vegetables. The wheat for the bread was milled in a nearby granary. Father Eric and his sisters visited the farm every Sunday, and he loved every-thing there—the cows, horses, goats, cats, and dogs. He especially loved his grandmother's freshly baked bread, slathered with the jams and jellies she made.

Father Eric was the youngest of eleven. Before long, his older siblings began to start families and his grandmother was at one point cooking and baking for twenty-three. And so the oven was always hot and there was always warm bread cooling on a rack. His mother began making the bread too, and she would send it with him for lunch at school.

In first grade, Father Eric's classmates brought lunches that included sandwiches made with store-bought bread. He discovered that he liked that bread, and asked his mother to start sending him with store-bought bread instead of her homemade kind. Here, Father Eric and I walked down the same path. We both feel sorry now that we demeaned our mothers' talents. I would give anything to be able to go back and eat one more slice of that delicious bread and tell her exactly how good it tasted.

The Golden Shawl

I, the youngest, was to be the last one to view my mother before the oak lid was closed and locked.

I took off the shawl I was wearing and was about to wrap it around my mother's shoulders when my brother held my wrist and said, "Don't. You'll need to wear it at the cemetery. It'll be very cold there."

At that moment, the mortician said, "No more time," and with that, the lid slammed down with an awful clang. So loud that the mourners in the back rows turned their heads, thinking something had fallen.

The clang and its echoes only partially masked the sound of my sobs.

The shawl had been from India, woven with silk threads so fine that even though it measured forty-eight inches by sixty, it could be folded into a size smaller than a woman's handkerchief. It had a tree of life pattern. When I was a child, my mother had explained that the pattern symbolized undying love. The threads of the shawl were of muted colors: crimson, purple, and orange. When the sun shone, it glowed golden and kept the sun's heat.

In my dreams, it still warms my mother's bones.

My Parents and Pies

Now I'm dreaming about my parents and pies.

In today's dream, I'm talking to my childhood friend, Florence, telling her how the sunny weather may change so my mother can take a walk while we can still see the rocks and ridges in our woods. I have to go now, I tell her. The clouds have moved in.

Now my father joins us as we climb into an old car. It's not in good condition, and its color has faded to a tired green. I don't know the model or the year and it's dilapidated, but I'm sure I'll be able to drive it.

Our goal is to go to a diner that has the best pies, including rhubarb, my favorite. The diner is about twelve miles away. We have just enough time to make it there before it closes, but on the way, we get diverted by seeing a side road that will take us close to a beautiful meadow near a stream. When we do so, all of us are disappointed, for the meadow is brown and the stream has almost dried up.

I turn back to the main road. Will the diner still be open? When I pull into the parking lot, all of us are relieved because there isn't a CLOSED sign on the door. However, the hostess tells us there are no more pies of any kind!

As we leave, we accidentally set off an alarm, a bleeping noise. We start to scramble out. Everyone is pushing and shoving. I help my parents through the door, but it's raining and cold. I wrap my arms around my mother and pull her close to keep her warm.

Then my apartment door opens with a bang—it's a staff member from the dining room. When the door opens, I smell freshly baked bread as my mother took it from the oven, as well as the aroma of the pie my mother always put in the oven right after the bread. I've wrapped my arms around my pillow and my hands are cold. I'm hoping the person at my door has a piece of pie, but alas, it's only an English muffin.

Dreaming of a Bird

We hadn't spoken for ten years. She wouldn't return my phone calls; I never understood why.

I was hiking my favorite trail in the Shenandoah National Park, sitting on a large granite rock. The trail was steep, and I was amazed that I'd gotten that far without my walker or my cane. I'd taken off my sneakers to cool my feet.

A large beautiful blue bird flew past me and sat on the top branch of a dead tree.

I knew both the rock and the tree intimately from the many years I'd been coming here with my husband.

I knew that I would never see him again. But there was someone behind me.

Without looking around, I knew it was my dear childhood friend, a fellow bird lover.

We could hear the bird's beautiful song, but we couldn't see it.

"If I can put my sneakers on, I'll be able to sit higher and see the whole bird," I told her.

She placed both hands under my upper arms, being careful to avoid putting pressure on the metal rod that had been inserted after I broke my left arm. She then carefully moved closer to prevent me from falling backwards.

When I tried to move up and forward with her, with a start, I realized I was in a bed.

I looked around: I was in my bed in my apartment!

With tears on my cheeks, I wondered, *How many times can you lose one friend?*

Dreaming of Paris

My dreams inspire me and at times console me, but sometimes they perturb me.

In one recent dream, I was the mother of two young teenagers, one a boy, the other a girl. We had returned to Paris for what somehow I knew would be our last time. The three of us could take our time and see the city thoroughly because we had six weeks before we had to leave. We did that, but in time we became somewhat bored. Then, by chance, we ran into a friend who'd never been to Paris.

And then suddenly, there was not enough time. We guided the woman as we retraced our steps. Underground and above ground as well. We returned to our favorite places. The Louvre and Notre Dame, of course, and through the little alleys that we'd seen many times before. All looked fresh once again.

Some days were sunny, other days it was rainy and dreary. And sometimes the weather changed midday, and we became drenched. We loved it all.

In the midst of our laughter, I woke to the sound of metal clanging. What was that? Oh yes, it must be the *éboueurs* (the garbage men) working very early in the morning.

I sat up and looked at the clock, teary-eyed with disappointment to be awake and out of the dream. It was not quite 4:00 a.m.

My Mother and Patt

Each June morning in 1947, my older sister Patt got up at 4:30 a.m. to gather the equipment so as to be ready to paint our barn when first light of morning hit the silo. First thing she did was lean two ladders against the barn, a metal extension ladder and a wooden ladder lashed together by rope so she could reach the highest edge of the barn wall.

Her painting schedule followed the sun; she timed it so she'd be working in the barn's shadow when the sun reached its zenith. And when that shadow became so dense that she couldn't see well, she'd climb down the extension ladder, swing over to the handmade wooden ladder, and once on the ground, begin cleaning her brushes.

Mother got up at the same early hour to fill the coffee pot so she could drink her coffee before she began the tortuous process of forcing down my swollen-throat liquid penicillin, then the even more dreaded cod-liver oil I had advanced scarlet fever that summer, so this exhausting routine continued for months.

But I like to imagine my mother and Patt, in that small kitchen of our simple farmhouse, clicking their cups in the gray dawn light, wishing each other a good day.

My Father's Hands

In the musical *Carousel*, Billy Bigelow, during his one-day leave from Purgatory, has his wish granted to see his wife, Julie, living a good life on earth.

When he does appear, unseen by everyone else, Julie knows he's there by her side.

When I lived in Manhattan many years ago, I'd get up about 5 a.m. on weekend days, grab a cup of coffee, and head to Central Park. I'd enter at 72nd Street and head north, walking fast. Skirting by the Sailboat Pond, I'd walk to 103rd Street, about forty blocks—more if you counted the blocks from my building before I entered the park.

There were frustrations as I strode through the park—dogs fighting or angrily barking, folks talking on their cellphones—but when I entered the Conservatory Garden at 101st Street, all was peaceful. It was my haven. I left all my worries and frustrations behind when I stepped through the tall, beautifully decorated cast-iron gates.

One morning, as usual, I stopped at a stand inside the park to pick up my second cup of coffee and a donut. As I leaned forward and up to pay the cashier, I suddenly felt lightheaded and stumbled back. A kind stranger righted me, and with the help of a second stranger, guided me to a nearby bench.

They called over a security guard.

"Should I call 911?" she asked.

"No, thanks. If you could help me to the street where I can catch a cab, I'll be fine."

With the help of a second security guard, they got me up the steep, uneven steps out of the park, called a cab, and helped me in.

"Where to?" the cab driver asked. "I can't hear you, speak up!"

I leaned forward as far as I could and gave him my address.

"You don't look good," he said.

When we drew up to my building, he tapped his horn twice and signaled to the doorman.

The doorman opened the door and helped me out. I couldn't move. He signaled to the other doorman.

"I think we should call 911."

I shook my head no.

They helped me to the elevator, and one helped me to my door.

I grabbed the walls to keep upright as I struggled to get to my son's room, where I collapsed onto the bed.

I wished I had my cell with me. I hadn't carried it with me that day, fearing I'd be mugged.

There was no way for me to get to the master bedroom, where my husband was still sleeping. I slumped down and rested my head on a hard bolster pillow. I had a terrible headache, and my chest hurt.

I was always told by my family, friends, and doctors that I just needed to relax.

A few years later, after going through extensive tests, I was told that it had nothing to do with my state of mind, but rather my anatomy.

The heart is like a car battery. If the electrical wires don't connect properly, the battery misfires and the car doesn't move, but just sits there shuddering.

My cardiac electrical wires were very close together, and physical stress could cause one to hit the other, causing the heart to beat at an alarming rate. I could have died with any one of those beats.

But, of course, I didn't know that. I tried relaxing. Nothing. I began to pray. I didn't want to die alone. I began to cry. My crying turned to sobs.

Then I felt someone behind me, and a hand touched my shoulder.

It was my father. He'd never been a consoling man in my life. That fell to my mother and sisters. And he had died decades earlier, no longer able to criticize or comfort.

"Don't be afraid. Whether you live or die, you'll be okay," he said, and rubbed my right shoulder. He kept his hand resting there.

I relaxed, and soon fell asleep.

I woke when my husband, concerned that I hadn't returned from my walk, opened the door.

He came around and took my hands.

"Your left hand is cold, but your right is warm! How can that be? And there's a dent in that pillow! Who's been here?"

I started to say "Dad," but thinking how weird that would sound, I said, "I'm not sure. Would you please get me a glass of water?"

The Skater's Waltz

As I began to get ready for the day, my classical music station announced it would play Strauss's complete *The Skater's Waltz*.

A challenge! See if I can be ready by the time the piece ends.

As I wash my face and rub on lotion, I relax and listen carefully.

As the music continues, I'm skating again.

Down the river on my childhood farm, at a pond at my brother's place near Chicago, with Peter on the rink in Central Park.

I pull on my tights, tug my tee shirt down over my head.

Will I get my shoes tied before the last note?

Magnolia Blossoms

1. The climate was too cold for magnolia trees to thrive in South Dakota, where I grew up. The first magnolia blossom I saw was at my sister's home near St. Louis. I was staying with her that summer, earning money to go to college.

When I entered the house for the first time and looked out toward the patio, I saw a tree with bare branches but holding the most beautiful white blossoms. I picked a blossom and carried it back to my bedroom, wanting to examine it more closely, and put it in a glass of water.

My sister called for me to come to the kitchen. When I returned, my five-year old nephew was jumping on the bed, a never-do from my sister. In an effort to get to him, I knocked the flower and the glass it was sitting in onto the floor.

In attempting to get him ready for school, and me ready for work, I left the mess on the floor.

When I did return, I found that the petals, now an ugly brown, were glued to the floor and had an odor. On the weekend, I walked to the patio to admire the blossoms more, but knew not to pick one.

2. A few years later, when I was living on the Upper East Side of New York City, I was riding the bus home from work up Madison Avenue. As the bus drove past the back of St. Patrick's Cathedral, I looked out the window and glimpsed for a few seconds magnolia blossoms against the rough dark gray stones of the cathedral's outer wall. From that angle, I couldn't see the trunk or the bark of the tree.

Curious, that weekend, I walked long blocks south to see the tree more closely. To my amazement, there was no trunk but only branches growing directly from the stone. I entered St. Patrick's on the 5th Avenue side and approached an usher. He explained that the granite outer wall had been built abutting the marble facade of the building, blocking the tree. But the tree's tendrils, seeking sunshine, had grown out through crevices in the mortar of the wall and become strong enough to bear blossoms.

Another time, a few years later, I was riding the bus to work at a different job when I heard one young woman say to another, "I hate this time of year! And I hate this sunny day. It depresses me!"

Her friend said, "What do you think about those blossoms?" gesturing to a magnolia tree by the side of the road.

She said, "I hate them too. When it rains, they smell like dog shit."

A week or so later, the two women stepped onto the bus, and I noticed the woman who'd said she hated magnolias was limping. As she passed my seat, I looked at her with sympathy and said, "Oh, what happened?"

She said, "I was hurrying to work, and I slipped on those damn blossoms. I'm going to petition the landlord to cut all those trees down."

Her friend said, "Oh, that won't do anything, they'll just grow back up!"

The first woman said, "By that time, I'll be living in a different area. One that doesn't have magnolia trees!"

3. Another time, I discovered the beauties of Conservatory Garden in Central Park. The staff offered a series of walking tours designed to highlight the blossoms of each season. I made sure that I was there the weekend they were talking about magnolia trees. On the tour, I learned that there are several varieties. The St. Patrick's tree was a saucer magnolia, which has blossoms that stay out only a very short time before they fade and drop. But there are many others, including star magnolias. I was fortunate to

be there on a weekend when the star magnolias were in full bloom. Even by the time my son and I left and we went back for a final look, some of the petals had fallen.

4. Every summer or fall, I made a trip to visit my brother Bill's house near Chicago. His wife's favorite flower was the saucer magnolia, and they had two large trees in their backyard. One year, it had turned very hot. The blossoms came out. Then, during my visit, it turned damp and rainy, with wind. When I stepped into his backyard, a terrible odor made me retch. It was the fallen, decaying magnolia blossoms. Back in the house, my brother told me he wanted to get rid of the magnolia trees, but because it was his wife's favorite flower, he was going to find other flowers that wouldn't smell—perhaps dahlias. He called the nursery and asked, "Does the dahlia stink as much as the magnolia?"

The salesperson said, "No, it has the most beautiful odor when it just opens."

On my visit two years later, I looked at the table that usually had a bouquet of magnolia flowers and it was bare. I said, "Bill, where are your flowers?"

He said, "I'm saving it for you." And he brought in a huge dahlia blossom. The most beautiful scent wafted through the room.

Love at First Sight

During her junior year of college, Joy signed up for a cruise sailing from eastern Canada. The roster was composed of a mix of college kids from all over. Sam and Joy were a part of twenty students.

The first night on board, Sam was singing arias, easily mixing French and Italian, when he spotted Joy, her strawberry blond hair and fair complexion highlighted by a deep blue sweater and jeans.

Sam became so flustered, he missed a note and then couldn't find his place on the sheet music. He asked a friend to take his place so he could follow Joy to her table.

Joy was in awe of Sam's voice, but not his appearance. His hair was uncombed and his casual shirt wrinkled and none too clean.

The contract was incredibly flexible. At one point, Joy and another gal split off to tour Venice while Sam stayed in Naples. When the ship carrying Joy and her friend was due back in Naples port, Sam and his friends borrowed a skiff to ride out to meet them. Usually small coins were thrown on the deck of a returning ship. But Sam and his pal, hoping to make an unforgettable impression, wanted to throw gold coins instead.

They hurried and found a stand that would exchange US dollars for lire. Back at the dock, when the ship they believed was Joy's came in, they threw the coins. But the deck shifted and the coins skittered down to the bottom of the sea. The young men were appalled.

Turned out, it wasn't even Joy's ship—her friend had given the young men the wrong information. They arrived twenty minutes later. The gals waved innocently. The guys grabbed two bouquets of flowers.

When telling this story, Sam looked at Joy and said, "If I had kept those gold coins, in today's exchange rate, I'd be a millionaire."

Joy looked at him and said to me, "There were many times when I was about to leave him. I'd grab a few things and be at the door, and then he'd start to sing. That always brought me back, and now we've been married fifty-four years. Or fifty-five. I can't remember."

Two Birthday Songs

I pause listening to Aaron Copland's "Appalachian Spring" to sing and record my off-key version of "Happy Birthday" to my grandson, Theo.

It's a special birthday, his thirteenth. He's a teenager now—well on his way to being a man.

Aaron Copland's song pays tribute to Appalachia, which holds one of my favorite places, Shenandoah National Park: very small in size, but its peaks and valleys hold a large variety of nature's offerings.

My husband, Joe, took me there the first spring we were married.

A few years later, pregnant with my older son, Peter, on Mother's Day, I was given my first blessing as a mother at Mass in the little church in the valley.

Each spring, we returned. Three years later, our second son, Steve, joined us.

Now Peter, Theo's father, continues the tradition: each spring retracing the trails we hiked, watching the same night sky, ordering the same wild blueberry ice cream.

Now that I'm no longer able to make that trip, Theo will do it in my stead, taking photos and videos recording the views and the sounds. And once more, I'll be back in that very special place.

Another

Landmark Lost

Ever since 1965, when I first moved to Manhattan, I've been tuning in to the WQXR newscast, a brief daily insertion of news into the New York City classical music station's regular repertoire. When RFK was assassinated, I was listening to WQXR and I heard a long period of static and strange yells. I thought the station wasn't working, but it turned out to be live coverage of the shooting and the aftermath. On 9/11, I couldn't get the TV to work, so I turned on WQXR. Somehow they found soothing music to play following the newscast, including the Adagio movement from Mozart's 23rd piano concerto and Mendelssohn's "On Wings of Song."

Last Friday, I was disappointed that there was no newscast. But I thought perhaps it was because the traffic was bad—the UN General Assembly was meeting—and the newscaster couldn't make it in time.

But this morning, the longtime announcer said, "Because some listeners are confused, I want to state unequivocally that the newscast has been permanently disbanded."

My heart dropped! The combination of the music and the newscast kept my psyche above ground during the dreadfully lonely pandemic, and the countdown to the day when my friends and I could be vaccinated. And when I contracted COVID and was in quarantine, the station played a similar role. There's nothing else like that wonderful combination of blissful music broken by stark reality.

PART 6:

Friends and

Community

My fellow residents here are interesting and often surprising. Remarkably, three (out of a quickly diminishing number) of us served in the Peace Corps in Thailand during the same years, though we never met there.

And three of my women friends here were traversing the same streets and avenues in Manhattan where I did my errands. One of them gave birth to her daughter and son at the same hospital where my sons were born.

We saw the same Broadway shows, went to the same concerts at Carnegie Hall, and shopped (or at least window-shopped) at Bergdorf, Saks, and Tiffany. Our kids played ball and sledded down the same slopes in Central Park.

And then there is Gunter, born in Schleswig-Holstein, as my grandfather was. His apartment is across the hall from mine. If we meet as we begin our day, Gunter raises his hand to his forehead, in a courtly pantomime of doffing his hat, and gives a small bow.

His gray hair and full beard are reminiscent of my Grandpa Bert, as are his gray-blue eyes. His stride is long and indicates that there's work to be done. In this case, food to be eaten! As with my grandfather, no time is ever wasted.

If I'm seated in the dining room in the morning before Gunter is, as he enters he gives me a wide smile and a thumbs-up. I return it. Silently we communicate, "We made it through another night!"

With all these connections and echoes, the friends I've made at my facility often feel like very longtime friends indeed, even though I've been here for only just over a year. And thank goodness. We lean on each other, forming a community that, although not without its stresses, provides comfort, entertainment, stability. Loneliness can be life-ending, and since I've been here, I've seen how hard people work to find connection: with each other, with the staff here, and sometimes, even, with animals and imaginary friends.

Sitting by the Eighth-Floor Elevator

Knitters with their creations, laughing, quickly exit
Stan's operatic arias fill the room from the phone
in his pocket
In the library, Joy and Sam discuss what are the real
rules of the bridge game they're playing
Juan whizzes by, then whizzes back shaking his head
More guests tonight than he'd been told
Joy heads to the elevator and her office to work
Sam heads to the activity room
Karen and Barbara retreat to the library
where they share a cup of coffee and a Danish
The scent of cinnamon overcomes the odor of
old french fries

Stan retreats, the glorious notes of the diva jiggling
in his jeans pocket
Sid strides purposely to the mailboxes
Returns, in the same manner, to the elevator
Elevator doors open and close
Sheldon arrives, tries to wend his way to a table
Walkers collide
Tempers do also
The women begin to arrive
Children tumble out

Merrily rushing to the grab basket
Giggly as they make their choices
Now grandparents arrive and cheers of delight drown
out all conversations
The elevator doors release another batch of children
Newcomers look baffled
Door opens and John S. booms, "Where's the alcohol?"

Someone grabs the TV remote and turns the volume
way up
Football! Washington Capitals!
The fans won't lower the volume but raise it instead
Complete pandemonium
All the while
The elevator doors open and open
Releasing happy passengers
Daniel, weaving gracefully, places glasses of wine and
drinks on tables
No need to give your order, he knows
Conversations now must be shouted
Happy hour has begun!

The poet retreats to the dining room to enjoy the glorious sunset in quiet.

A Night at the Onyx Theater

The heavy door is propped open.

VOICES IN THE ROOM: Go on in, now's the time to
grab your seat!
Hmm, that's a good smell!
It's a popcorn night!
Get me some, please.
There's no cup.
Oh, I'll get one.
Get two.
Oh, I forgot to pick up a pillow.
Don't worry, I'll get one for you.
Are you sleeping?! Before the movie has even begun?
No, I was just resting my eyes.
You were snoring!
Well, I was snoring while I was awake. I often do that.
Whatever!
Good evening, your honorable Dr. Bob. Will you
please move your big feet so I can get to my seat?
You're going to watch a movie with us?
I'll give it ten minutes.

FROM THE DOORWAY: Is there a movie tonight?

CHORUS: Yes.

VOICES IN THE ROOM: Come on in and set yourself down.
What's the movie?

Long pause with a lot of paper rustling.

No, that was last night! You're looking at the wrong sheet.

Oh, it doesn't matter. If I don't like it, I'll just get up and leave.

You pulled the back of my seat! That hurt my neck!

I don't think I did, but, if so, I'm sorry.

Creaks and bangs and sighs as others take their places.

Excuse me! I have to get down to the front row.

Isn't it time for the movie to start? How long do we have to wait?

Five minutes pass. Four, three, two . . .

Wake up! *Concierge gently jostles a viewer.*

Eh! What?

The movie is starting!

Oh! I knew that!

Opening credits roll.

Enjoy the movie!

I can't hear it!

Volume increases.

That's too loud!

Trust me. It'll get better.

Door closes with finality. Murmurs and complaints continue with pleas for silence.

Ignore. The poet focuses on the impending onscreen mayhem.

Love in Many Forms

My assisted living facility was hosting a celebration of its second anniversary as an independent entity. Flyers asked the residents to dress for the occasion. There would be no T-shirts, no shorts! Even though I wasn't completely unpacked yet, I found a colorful shawl and tossed it over my shoulders, thus looking dressier than usual.

A loud noise hit me when I exited the elevator. Rock music was playing at full blast.

I managed to get around the crowd and over to the side where servers were passing out wine and hors d'oeuvres, but there was no way for me to take either of those and still keep my balance.

In a minute, fighting to be heard over the rock music, a jazz quartet started playing.

A tall man with dark hair came toward me and said, "Let me help you." He ushered me to the far corner of his table. At the table was a lovely woman with blond hair who smiled and nodded as I sat down. "I'm Paul," said the man. This was COVID time, so we just brushed wrists. "And this is Dorothy."

Paul asked the band to play Dave Brubeck's "Take Five."

Residents and their friends talked louder and louder.

Amid the chaos, Paul somehow snared champagne for the three of us. "We're celebrating Dorothy's eighty-second birthday this evening!" he said.

"You don't look anywhere near that age," I said to her. "How did the two of you meet?"

"Oh, we've known each other for thirty or so years," Paul said.

"Thirty-three to be precise," Dorothy interjected.

Paul continued. "Four of us were good friends: Dorothy, her boss, Patty, Patty's husband Dr. Steve, and me. We all love movies. On the weekends, we would go to the movies to decompress. During the week, because our office buildings were right next to each other, we would meet at lunch to walk on the mall. We walked even when it was raining and cold. We'd come prepared with ponchos.

"One of my favorite memories is when Washington was offering T-shirts, four for four dollars, in order to encourage people to visit all the monuments. Dorothy insisted that each week we visit a new T-shirt stand to get each of the four designs. She always bought size large so she could wear them to bed. She still wears them."

Later I learned that Paul doesn't live at Brightview, that he lives independently in Bethesda but still visits his dear friend Dorothy every morning and night to check that she has taken her medicine. In his seventies, Paul still plays softball; he throws the ball faster than anyone on the team. At Brightview, he and Dorothy have continued their movie-going habits, visiting the theater almost every night. At times, when Dorothy becomes too tired to continue watching, even though Paul wants to see the movie, he gently helps her back to her room.

Hidden Bottles

After dinner, Danny and Leon bring two cans of ginger ale as I'd requested, but no water.

"But you forgot—" I start to say.

In unison they start to walk away, but then stop, and with straight faces, begin pulling bottle after bottle out of their apron pockets, deliberately placing them right in front of me.

Slight smiles are on their faces as they exit, and just before they enter the kitchen, I see them high-fiving.

Cranes

The dining room in my facility has a wall of windows looking out over downtown Bethesda. And often, because of ongoing construction, there are two, three, four, and even five cranes on the horizon—one time, it's rumored, someone saw *six*. I was fascinated by the cranes from my first morning there. They dominated the skyline. I watched the hoists go up and down, transporting concrete, and I watched the men balance on very small railings. I'm very acrophobic, so I had to turn away when the men would lean over the side to pull the rigging in.

For a while, cranes were the main topic of conversation at lunch each day. The men worked in 103-degree heat; they worked when it was very cold and rainy. Everyone was concerned about their safety. I asked the activity director if someone who worked with cranes for one of the construction companies could speak to us and answer the residents' questions. She thought that was a good idea, but it took her a long time to find the right person. When he came, he spoke to me first, making sure he'd be ready with the answers people would want to know.

He explained that the first thing to go up in any construction project was the crane itself, piece by piece. When the project was finished, the last thing to be taken down, piece by piece, was the crane.

The day after the crane man talked, the women at the round table in the dining room—who hadn't gone to the meeting—started asking questions about what that crane was doing out there. Why were there men out there? When were they ever going to be done with it? I told them that the crane man had explained all that. They said they hadn't come because they weren't interested in hearing about all that machinery and engineering stuff. So instead I explained it to them and other residents who had been there explained it to them also. The discussion went on for about two weeks until somebody's illness became the topic we all discussed.

Another time, I saw a woman enter the dining room, but pause at the door.

"Are they here today?!" she called.

"Who? Your family?" someone said.

"No, my boyfriend."

"Who's your boyfriend?"

"The crane," she said, gazing out the window. "Have they taken him away?"

"No one takes it," someone said. "It can move by itself."

"Oh. He didn't say goodbye."

"Cranes don't talk, you know."

"Well, he could have nodded. Are they all gone?"

"No. Look behind you."

"Oh, there he is!" the woman cried happily. "I recognize him by the writing on his side."

"That's the name of the company that owns him," said the other resident, then hit the table. "Owns 'it,' I mean. Now you have me talking like you!"

"Is that bad?" said the woman, coming to sit down. "Now where's my menu?!"

The Parrot

Four women sitting at a round table.

WOMAN ONE: I'd love to have a pet here.

WOMAN TWO: What kind?

WOMAN ONE: A cat. Not just one. One would be lonely. Two or three. So they could play together. *Looking at the woman across the table.* Do you have a pet?

WOMAN THREE: Yes, I have a bird. It's the size of a pigeon.

WOMAN ONE: Oh, a parakeet!

WOMAN THREE: No, not a parakeet! It's a Solomon Islands . . .

WOMAN TWO: You have a snake in your apartment?!

WOMAN THREE: No, listen before squealing.

WOMAN TWO: I didn't squeal! I was just reacting.

WOMAN THREE: Well, either way. Pay attention! Listen up! It's a Solomon Islands parrot.

WOMAN ONE: How big is it? How much does it weigh?

WOMAN THREE: Oh, about the size of a large pigeon. But its wingspan is about forty-eight inches.

WOMAN ONE: Is it a man or a woman?

WOMAN THREE: You mean male or female.

WOMAN ONE: Yes, my mistake. Sorry!

WOMAN FOUR: You don't need to apologize. The parrot isn't here, and it can't hear you.

WOMAN ONE: Does he talk? How many words?

WOMAN THREE: Somewhere around forty-eight to sixty. Depending on how he feels.

WOMAN ONE: You mean he has moods?

WOMAN THREE: Of course. And his feathers are beautiful—all the colors of a rainbow! This is the only species of parrot where the male's plumage is more colorful than the female's.

> *Before anyone can answer, she pulls out*
> *her cellphone and opens her photo album.*

ALL BUT WOMAN THREE: Amazing! Beautiful! What's his name?

WOMAN THREE: Oliver.

WOMAN ONE: Oh, like the Charles Dickens character.

WOMAN THREE: I don't know anything about Charles Dickens. I just liked the name: Oliver.

WOMAN ONE: Can I visit him?

WOMAN THREE: Yes, just knock on my door. It'll take some time for me to put him in his cage, so don't run away when I don't open it right away.

WOMAN ONE: My running days are over.

WOMAN THREE: And now there's another Oliver! My nephew called the other day. He asked my permission to name his son Oliver.

WOMAN ONE: That would be your grandnephew.

WOMAN THREE: Whatever. I never had any time for this great- and grand- stuff.

WOMAN ONE: What did you say?

WOMAN THREE: He didn't need to ask me. It's just a name.

WOMAN ONE: Just a name?! A person's name is the most important thing each of us have!

All make murmuring sounds of agreement.

WOMAN THREE: Well, I have to go now. Find a to-go carton and get some chicken for Oliver.

WOMAN ONE: What kind of food does Oliver eat? Bird food?

WOMAN THREE: That stuff is garbage! It doesn't have the minerals a parrot needs. I feed him people food. Chicken, fish. I tried hamburger once, but he spat it out.

WOMAN ONE: Is he grateful? Does he say "thank you?"

WOMEN THREE: Oh, yes. Over and over. Until I say, "Cut it out!" Then he says that over and over. Then I say, "Enough!!" Once I went and said the *F* word. The next morning an aide came in early. It was still dark. She said I had to get dressed right away. There was no way I was going to get dressed at that hour.

I kept resisting. Oliver knew I was getting very upset, and he yelled, "Get the *F* out!"

Everyone laughs.

WOMAN ONE: I guess it would be worth getting a parrot just for that.

All agree.

WOMAN THREE: When you visit my room, don't wear anything that's red.

WOMAN ONE: Like a matador.

WOMAN THREE: Oliver is not mad! How dare you say that!

WOMAN ONE: I didn't say "mad." I said "matador." Like in Spain, where the men fight the bulls. He flashes his red cape. Bulls hate anything that's red.

Woman one picks up her spoons and begins to play the "Toreador Song" by hitting them together. When she finishes, the other women at the table shout, "Olé!"

WOMAN ONE: Does Oliver like people?

WOMAN THREE: Would you like to meet him?

WOMAN ONE: Would Oliver bite me if I'm wearing red?

WOMAN THREE: No, but he might nip you with his beak. Be sure you knock on the door before you enter. Then I'll put Oliver in his home.

WOMAN ONE: You mean a cage?

WOMAN THREE: No, not a cage! It's a large beautiful antique basket. Chinese. Japanese. One of those far-away places. Come. We'll go to my room together.

WOMAN ONE: No thanks, I'm going to Dr. Bob's talk.

WOMAN TWO: I have work to do.

WOMAN FOUR: I like to see birds. On the other side of the glass.

The parrot woman leaves, to-go cup in hand.
The others continue to eat.

Too Damn Much Rain!

It's been raining every day for the last six weeks! Torrents of rain and gusty wind. Tornadoes are forecast day by day. Occasionally, a bit of sun peeks out from a dark cloud, but before spirits have time to lighten, rain returns. People entering the building try to stand under the awning to shake off their umbrellas, but the kids are impatient and dance their way in, leaving puddles of water on the tile floors. CAUTION signs are placed strategically around, and concierges grab mops to make the floor safe again. Residents, staff, and visitors all are affected. Dogs yelp and growl, warning their owners of impending danger after the lightning strikes.

"It can't go on forever," the optimists say.

But we more pessimistic ones say, "Are you sure about that?! It's already surpassed Exodus's forty days."

The Birthday Cake

that Crashed

I ordered an extra-large birthday cake to celebrate my eighty-fifth. Large enough for residents, their relatives, and staff to have seconds.

It was to be the size of a third of a card table. I chose the icing to be pink, orange, and purple flowers, and a candle of the same colors.

When I saw it in person for the first time, I was astounded. It was spectacular, and the birthday candle shimmered in the dining room lights.

My two sons, my grandson, and my daughter-in-law, Laura, joined me in admiring it, but then a server came to the table. She was crying—literally!

Over sobs we heard her saying, "I'm sorry. I'm sorry."

"What are you sorry about?" I asked.

"Your cake is ruined!"

"It looks fine to me."

"We had it all set up," she said. "Everything was perfect on the table, the napkins, the silver, the ice bucket for wine, the cake. We went to the kitchen. But as I came back down the hallway, I saw a woman grab a fork, take a piece of the cake, and begin to eat it. I told her, 'No! You can't do that. That's Barbara's birthday cake.' She wasn't convinced. It took another waitress before she walked away."

I said, "I can't see anything wrong."

"Look at it carefully," she said. "There are the marks that she made with the fork."

I said, "I don't see any missing piece."

"I took it out and scrunched it together so it wouldn't look so bad."

"The Japanese don't like anything to be too perfect," I told her. "They call it wabi-sabi—imperfect beauty."

She said, "That makes me feel better." She went to the kitchen and brought out some drinks. The director of food services had ordered the best Sauvignon Blanc and the best bourbon, and the servers poured us cups.

My family stood up and toasted my eighty-fifth!

The news had just come in that President Joe Biden had bowed out of the election.

My son Peter said, "Mom, this is a day to remember."

His son Theo said, "Unlike 9/11, which was sad, this will be a happy day to remember."

Everyone said, "Here's to Mom on her eighty-fifth and to President Biden for his humility and graciousness!"

Cheers all around.

Then the staff and the residents sang "Happy Birthday," and I tried to blow out the candles. For some reason, there were three candles. On my first try, no luck. Then Steve held me up so I could be on the same level as the candles. On the second try, nothing. At this point, everyone was cheering, "You can do it! You can do it!" I finally blew the candles out and everyone cheered. I told the staff to offer a slice of cake to everyone there. After cake, we adjourned to the library on the same level to open gifts. Theo gave me a very thoughtful drawing set. Sadly, my son's wife Katee could not be there. Her birthday is the same day as mine, but her mother's is two days later. She usually wraps gifts perfectly. But when I looked at hers and Steve's, there was packing tape on both of them.

I looked at Steve and said, "Did you wrap these?"

He said, "Mom, I tried to take them through security, but neither of them would pass. The guard took his knife and just opened both of them. I said, 'Don't, don't!' I was very upset. So they called the chief of security. I said, 'You just can't keep ripping things open. They are birthday gifts for my mother. It's her eighty-fifth birthday.'

"So the chief said, 'Okay, let's see what's in there.'"

One was a glasses holder with a metal bottom for

balance. The other was a night lamp with two batteries rattling around and a steel base that could've been dangerous. Finally the chief let them go through. Steve asked if they had any tape to put the boxes back together, and they gave him the packing tape.

We were all laughing about this for a long time.

A group that I knew loved sweets was sitting at the two middle tables in the dining room. I said to the server, "Can you please offer more cake to the group sitting at the middle tables in the dining room?"

It was three men who loved sweets and four women who loved chocolate sweets. At first, they each took one slice, but I said, "There's plenty more. Please come over and take some back with you." I had brought boxes and the server did a beautiful job of cutting a double portion of the cake into the boxes. One woman asked for a "double *double*" of chocolate.

The server said, "I don't know if I can do that," but he tried, and it went perfectly. We all cheered, and the server took the cake back to the kitchen.

My family left that night. It was a Sunday, and I had promised slices of cake to a number of staff who were coming in on Monday. In the morning, I asked where the cake was.

Everyone said it wasn't there, but they didn't know why. Finally, I found the server from the night before and he said, "It's gone, but I can't tell you what happened."

I said, "What? Why can't you tell me?"

Finally, he said he would tell me. "Last night, we were taking your cake downstairs to the freezer in the basement. We had rolled it into the elevator on a cart. Partway down, the doors opened and a visitor came in. As the guy stepped in, he shook the elevator, and the cake smashed right into him!"

I said, "Isn't there any left?"

The server said, "Not a bite."

Turns out, this cake was a true example of wabi-sabi.

The Strawberry Moon

June 2024 would have two full moons, and meteorologists reported that in the Northern hemisphere, the penultimate one would be the brightest and reddish in color. That night it would be the lowest to the horizon that it had been for decades; it wouldn't be in that position again for almost a century.

That night I was in Bethesda, MD. My oldest son, Peter, and his family were in DC. For both of us, buildings blocked our views of the horizon at 8:30 p.m., the best viewing time.

My younger son, Steve, and his wife, Katee, were at their home in upstate NY. The best viewing time there was in the middle of the night—too late an hour for them to wait up. But at the moon's zenith, the bright light woke them up.

I wanted someone I knew to witness this miracle of nature, so I called a few friends who lived in the narrow swath that reached from eastern Massachusetts to North Carolina.

My older brother, Bob, who is eighty-seven, often reminds me that his home in Minot, ND, is much closer to the top of the earth than where I live. I left Bob a voicemail.

He picked it up while he, his ninety-two-year-old girlfriend, Phyllis, and her seventy-five-year-old son-in-law were celebrating their birthdays in the best steakhouse in the region, a twenty-minute drive from Minot. When Bob played the voicemail out loud, they all said, "What are we waiting for?"

They rushed out of the restaurant carrying their coffee and dessert. In the car, they checked online to find the best vantage points to view the moon, and learned that the full moon would be at its lowest to their east—the Strawberry Moon would be later and be at their west.

They drove three and a half miles to a hospital parking lot on the edge of Minot, where they observed and marveled.

They had to get out of the car and walk up a steep slope in order to see the horizon, and the weather that had been unusually cold turned colder. Wind blew gusts into their faces, and then an icy rain began to pelt them. They continued to stand. When they returned to the car, they had to walk back down the slope. This path was very rocky, and it was a struggle to stay upright.

The next day I called Bob. "Did you have any luck?" I asked him.

He described the night to me, and I thought about astronaut John Glenn's quote: "To look out at this kind of creation out here and not believe in God is to me impossible."

Back in the car heading home, Bob told me, they had all agreed that even though they had never been colder before, the night of the Strawberry Moon had been the best night in all of their long lives.

The Winter Gardener

Even as a child, my brother Bill loved plants—plants that grew fruit and plants that produced blossoms. Between the rows of green beans in our farm garden, Bill planted marigolds, whose scent deterred moths. As a young adult and a new husband, he planned ahead and brought bags of the best soil from our land to his new home in New Ulm, Minnesota. Using peach crates and plywood boards, he nailed together small planters that he hung along the outside staircase leading to his second-floor apartment. In those, he planted cucumbers, petunias, and geraniums. As the summer progressed, anyone entering his apartment would have to step carefully so as not to crush the plants.

Two years later, he and his wife, Ruth, moved to a small cul-de-sac northwest of Palatine, Illinois. Before they purchased the house, Bill went there early in the morning and late in the afternoon to make sure his plants would have the right amount of light. A couple years later, fearing that developers would rob him of this light, he purchased an additional property next to his own.

His business required him to travel overseas extensively, and to stay for long periods of time. During that time, Ruth "volunteered" to move hoses and hoe weeds. As their three children grew older, they were recruited. All of the family loved the produce but resented having to do the chores. Bill thought—to give them some incentive—he'd give them peppers and tomatoes. The children went door to door charging ten cents per tomato and twenty cents per pepper. With that, they learned responsibility and time-management.

Bill bought another few acres a quarter mile away from their house. He always gave away anything the family couldn't eat. Tacked to the back of a cupboard door, he kept a list of neighbors who preferred different vegetables. When years and years later he moved to an assisted care facility, he still had that list and he took it with him.

When I visited him in 2017, in a new, bigger house he'd bought with a large garden, he recruited me early in the morning to pick the crop before the sun could do its damage. Again, I tried to skip over petunia blossoms on my way to the tomato patch. He always researched new and interesting varieties and would test them. So that year, when I was there, the cherry tomatoes were trained up on stakes, above my waist. And below them, there were cucumbers, regular tomato plants, and jalapeno peppers.

Even though it looked like a delightful job, it was very hot, and the mosquitoes found me right away. And it was hard walking. I remember once I stumbled and he said, "Don't grab a stake!" I said, "What should I grab?"

At the time of my visit, Bill's wife had passed away and he had formed a warm relationship with Elsie, who also loved gardening. He told me, "Barbara, I have to run out. There'll be people stopping by to ring the doorbell. Don't be concerned, just ask who they are, and be sure to mark down how many tomatoes they took, how many cucumbers, and if they need anything else."

Sure enough, I was just relaxing and the doorbell rang. It was a policeman! I was scared to death something had happened to my brother. I said, "Oh my God, is Bill okay?"

The policeman said, "I'm sorry to bother you. I'm just here to pick up the vegetables. Tell Bill I have enough summer squash to last me for a while."

While I was visiting Bill, he asked me to help pack a FedEx box with tomatoes and cucumbers. It was for the family that had lived next door at his first house, who had now moved far away.

The following year, I called him and said, "What I'd like for my birthday is for you to FedEx *me* a box." So on my birthday he called and said, "You don't have it yet, but you will in two days."

I called the doorman and asked him if there was a box down there. He said, "There's a box but we can't read the address. It's leaking something red. And it smells!"

I said, "Can I pick it up?"

He said, "We'll bring it up on a cart."

I opened the door. The doorman put the box on the floor outside my apartment, took his blade, and opened the package. The box, soaked with tomato juice, collapsed. I managed to pull out from the bottom one plum tomato that had turned into sauce. When I poured it into a little dish, put a spoon in, and tasted it, it was the most divine tomato flavor I'd ever tasted.

Three years later, Bill moved into an assisted living facility. To him, one of the prime advantages of the place was that he'd be able to keep gardening. He rented a plot in a community garden a five-minute walk from the building—picking the plot with the best light—and planted asparagus, green beans, peas, beets, rhubarb, and tomatoes. Against the protestations of his daughters, he also planted a number of vegetables on the very small balcony outside his room. As before, he gave away the vegetables to his neighbors. The extras he took down to a community give-away table where, often, there was a line waiting for his produce.

Bill had always had beautiful amaryllises at home and when he moved to the assisted living facility, he brought one along in a Folger's coffee can and placed it on his balcony. He cared for it, keeping it trim. At Valentine's Day, all his hard work was rewarded: the amaryllis bloomed nine wondrous blossoms on two stems.

A Ghost on the Terrace

He didn't want to do it. But the accumulated two feet of snow and ice on the eighth-floor terrace outside the dining room at Brightview had begun to leak into the heating system, causing water damage in the apartments below. It was his job, as a certified plumber, to shovel away the snow outside.

It was terribly cold, about twelve degrees, with strong gusts of wind. The plumber's plan was to work for half an hour, then come in to warm up.

But he got caught up with chiseling the frozen snow off the terrace floor, so it was about forty minutes before he tried to push open a door that opened into a hallway next to the dining room. It opened only a foot or so, and then wouldn't budge!

He banged hard on the metal door, but the noise blended in with the noise the waitstaff was making carrying metal food warmers on metal trays. He jumped up to the small square window at the top of the door. But no one noticed him.

With great difficulty, slipping and falling several times, he made his way back over the icy wall of snow that he'd shoveled earlier. He moved into the sun to stay warm. As the sun moved around and the day grew darker, the shadows became icy. The man jumped up and down, windmilled his arms. Sometimes he sat down, but when he grew tired, he knew he had to keep moving, so he stood up again.

When he'd been out there for many hours, the residents returned for dinner. Through the window, he waved at a table of men who sat down nearby.

One man jumped.

"What's wrong?" his tablemate asked.

"I thought I saw a man out there."

"I see what you mean, but that's not a man. That's a shadow cast by the waiters moving around inside."

"Well, we know it's not a woman," said a woman seated at a nearby table. "No woman is stupid enough to be out in this weather."

"I'd go over and check, but my wheelchair won't let me," said one man.

The plumber finally reached the glass door.

"Oh my God, that is a person. Open the door right away!"

"These doors don't open. They're locked."

"Waiter! Waiter! Open the door! There's someone out there!"

"Don't be silly. No one would be out there in the freezing cold."

My tablemate and I had been discussing the sad news of a dear man who'd died earlier that day. Suddenly, she shivered and dropped her knife and fork with a clatter.

"I'm superstitious," she explained, as she pulled her sweater closer about her.

"No, it's true. I also felt a gust of cold, but it's over now."

The next morning, I learned that the poor guy had been out there from about noon until 6:30 p.m. Six hours! He could have died.

Once inside, rather than take time to warm up, he took the service stairs to the ground floor, eight flights of steep concrete steps.

Because his gloves were frozen and the bottoms of his boots covered with ice, he fell three times: gashing his head, hitting his knees, and slicing his hand. He refused an ambulance.

Downstairs, people tried to help get him out of his wet clothes and into a dry shirt and jacket and scarf. He said, "I don't want to get blood on your clothes." He didn't want to sit on the lobby couch because he didn't want to get blood on it. He had blood on his hands and was upset. "I want this blood off," he said. "I don't like looking at it." They brought paper towels, which didn't work. He tried to put a Band-Aid on it, and it didn't stop the bleeding. A waiter found two washcloths and tied them together to make a compression bandage, and that helped. There was so much blood on the lobby floor that they had to get a painter's tarp to cover it so people wouldn't slip.

Finally, his boss came and took him to the ER, where they stitched him up and did tests to make sure he was okay. He was there for two days.

The day following the incident, when I was telling my friends the story, I said, "I saw him only a minute, but with his glasses coated with snow and his face a mask of snow turned to ice, he looked like that photo of Shackleton at the North Pole. He looked like a ghost."

"And that's what he would have been in a few more minutes."

"A ghost, while we were sitting here complaining about our food!"

"Maybe we could complain less?"

"Where would the fun be in that?"

PART 7:

The Presence

of Death

L et us talk about death.

In an assisted living facility, death walks the halls with us from morning until night. We discuss death all the time, sometimes using black humor to cope. Other residents' longevity is a constant source of gossip. And then there are the ambulances. Ambulances come and go regularly, bearing our friends and fellow residents to the hospital, some of them never to return. We hear the sirens and see the trucks parked outside, and we see people going down in gurneys in the elevators.

The two elevators are conductors of death. Everyone knows that if a person is feeling okay, the paramedics only cover them with a white sheet, leaving their heads uncovered. If a person is really not okay, the paramedics hang a curtain around the gurney to shelter them from our sight. And then everyone talks about it in the dining room—speculating on whether someone will return or not, arguing over whether theirs was a life well-lived or not. We can't escape death, but somehow we never grow quite comfortable with it. And when our friends leave us, we grieve together.

Nowhere to Die

*A woman in front of the elevator holds the
door open, talking to two women inside.*

WOMAN HOLDING THE DOOR: A woman died last
night. In her room! I don't want to die all alone in
my room. That's nowhere to die.

*Finally she leaves for the dining room,
allowing the door to close. Inside the elevator:*

ONE WOMAN: I know what she means, but I hope she
doesn't die in here either.

OTHER WOMAN, *looking around the elevator*: I don't
know if there would be enough room for a body.

Something Sweet

Scene 1, A petite woman enters, chooses a table by the window, and sits in the exact spot she always shared with her husband before he passed away.

WOMAN: Is it Sunday?

WAITER: No, it's Friday.

She starts to get up.

WAITER: The choices are very good today.

WOMAN: No, no. It doesn't matter what the food is.

WAITER: Well, then, what?

WOMAN: The crane men will be working today.

WAITER: So?

WOMAN: That nearby crane may crash through the window. I can't stay here.

WAITER: But what about lunch?

WOMAN: I'll order the food delivered to my room.

Moving more quickly than usual, she heads to the elevator.

*Scene 2, Overheard from a
nearby dining room table.*

VOICES IN THE ROOM: The ambulance came last night!
For whom?
For Joe.

Why?
He fell. He'd never take assistance.
Well, he's proud.
Aren't we all?

*Scene 3, A resident stops by the second
round table in the dining room and says that
someone (not a resident) has died.*

VOICES IN THE ROOM: How old was he?

In his late sixties, maybe early seventies.

His brother died when he was only forty, and an uncle
died really young. Maybe late twenties.

His whole family was notorious for dying!

Gasps of shock around the table.

Well, we all have to go sometime. *Said with resignation.*

There's nothing we can do about that.

Silence.

CHEERY WAITRESS: Is everything all right here? You
ladies are unusually quiet tonight.

Silence continues.

Ready for something sweet?

Eulogy for Stew

My friendship with Stew began in a very inauspicious manner.

It was during the Q&A after I'd read a chapter of my book, *Lost Without the River*. The activity director was asking for opinions.

"What do you think? Did you like it? Let's get a show of hands."

Almost all of the group said they liked it, and raised their hands, and then lowered them. Stew raised her hand and kept it up.

"Stew, what's your opinion?"

"I hated it!"

I cringed.

"But why?!"

"It's boring! Everything moves so slowly!" Looking directly at me, she continued, "You keep describing trees, flowers, and the sky. Who cares about any of that!"

Unable to speak, I took a long sip of water. "Maybe we could discuss this at dinner tonight?" I suggested.

"I'd like that!" Stew replied.

I learned so much from my new friend.

At the time my son was very sick with COVID.

When I sat down at breakfast one morning, Stew said, with her usual candor, "You look terrible!"

"I didn't sleep well," I said, "I worried all night. My philosophy is if I worry enough, the bad thing I'm worrying about won't happen."

"That's ridiculous! In fact, it's one of the stupidest things I've ever heard! Worrying won't help one iota. Whatever is going to happen will happen. A person is born with a limited amount of time and energy," she continued. "You can't afford to waste any of that!"

I know that I learned more from her than she from me. But I do remember one time when I opened her view.

One of our differences was that Stew loved physical structures: the Chrysler and Empire State buildings, of course, but cabins and huts, bus stations and air terminals. She loved Penn Station! I hate it.

My primary love is the natural world. Stew did her best to ignore it.

"I don't like nature. I never waste my time looking at trees or flowers."

I determined to change her mind.

We were sitting in the activity room. It was late afternoon on an off-and-on sunny-cloudy day. We both had difficulty looking into bright light. Stew sat with her back to the windows. When a dark cloud dimmed the room, I turned, and at that very moment, a single beam of light hit the leaves on the magnolia tree outside, turning their faded leaves to a wondrous gold.

"Oh, Stew, this is one of the most amazing things I've ever seen. You can't miss this!"

As the wind flipped the leaves from their backs to their fronts, she turned, and I turned to look at her. Her face was aglow with a beautiful smile.

Stew lived a very active, dramatic life, moving from one apartment to another, from one house to another, from state to state. At times she was poor and hungry, and then she made a large fortune. Through all of that, she didn't have friends and was never happy.

"I didn't know what peace and happiness were," she told me, "but here, at Brightview, I have both: friends and peace. I love the residents, the kitchen and dining room crew, the nurses, the aides, I love them all!"

And we all loved Stew.

That's What Men Do

A dinner table of two men and three women.

WOMAN ONE: My husband owned a restaurant in DC.

WOMAN TWO: In Bethesda?

WOMAN ONE: No, in DC.

WOMAN THREE: And what does he do now?

WOMAN ONE: He's dead.

WOMAN THREE: Well, that's what men do!!

WOMAN TWO: You shouldn't have taken him to the hospital.

WOMAN ONE: Well, I didn't take him. I was in a class when he collapsed, and the nurse called for the ambulance.

WOMAN TWO: Well, I still say he wouldn't have died if he hadn't been in the hospital. Too many people die in hospitals.

MAN ONE: Of course. That's where very sick people go.

MAN TWO: How old was he?

WOMAN ONE: Ninety-two. He was going to be ninety-three in a week.

WOMAN THREE: Well, that's old.

WOMAN ONE: Not for me. My family has great genetics! My aunt lived until she was over one hundred!

WOMAN THREE: What about your uncle?

Woman one: He died young, very young.

Woman three: It sounds like the women live long, but the men don't.

Woman one: Well he's not a good example. He was in the army, and he was killed in the war. I never knew him, I was too young. My mother is still living.

Man two: Heavens! How old is she?

Woman one: 102. She's going to be 103 in a month.

Woman three: Well, I still think you shouldn't have taken your husband to the hospital.

Why We Live So Long Here

Three women talking in the theater.

WOMAN ONE: Who are those strange people taking those prime seats in the front row?

WOMAN TWO: I don't know. I've never seen them before.

WOMAN ONE: Well, if they don't live here, we should ask them to leave.

WOMAN THREE: They do belong here. And they do need to sit that close to the screen. The little woman on the left has been here for three years. She used to live on the seventh floor, but now she lives in Wellspring Village on the second floor.

WOMAN TWO: Why did she move?

WOMAN THREE: Her eyesight is very poor. She has macular degeneration and can't tolerate bright lights. So when the health aides turned on the lights to check on her, it was painful. In Wellspring Village, the lights have dimmers and the aides are trained. Do you remember the woman who used to walk with two extended canes, and the man who would help her get to her seat, and leave the theater?

WOMAN ONE: Are they married? Or is he her son?

WOMAN TWO: More like a grandson? He can't be anymore than thirty-five.

Woman three: No, he's sixty-five or sixty-six. He was working until just a few weeks ago.

Woman two: Well, who is that man and woman sitting next to them?

Woman three: All four are just friends from years ago! They are all film buffs! Ask them who the stars are in any old movie, and they'll be able to tell you. Also how old the actor was at the time the movie was made, and what other movies he or she performed in.

Woman two: Look here comes a really tall woman, and she's going to block my view!

Woman one: And the woman with her is going to block MY view.

Woman three: The shorter one is Virginia.

Woman one: Well she must be new. I've never seen her before!

Woman two: Is she married to the man next to her? He's MUCH younger!

Woman three: No, that is her son, and he's only a little older than her daughter.

Woman two: We sure have a lot of old people here.

Woman one: Seems like we do. And it seems that there are a lot of old men here. Is that unusual? (*Turning to a man behind her.*)

Man one: Statistically, women live longer than men. That's what I always thought.

WOMAN THREE: At a resident council meeting, they told us that they had researched this, and here, where we live, has the oldest residents, men and women, compared to other Brightview facilities. We have men here who are older than 102 and even 104. And we have a woman here who's 105. (*Turns to a second man.*) How old are you?

MAN TWO: I'm 104.

WOMAN TWO: We seem to be having more and more old people here. Why do you think that is?

WOMAN ONE: I think that's because we care for each other.

WOMAN TWO: That's true. You're always helping people. You roll the wheelchairs to the table, you stand up and move chairs for them. And you do this time and again: morning, noon, and night.

WOMAN ONE: Well, you do the same thing. You're always getting people's mail and bringing it to them, or getting the daily newsletter and bringing it to them. And pushing wheelchairs.

MAN ONE: And you do that for me, morning and night. And what do I say? I say, Merci.

WOMAN TWO: No matter what you say, I love you.

MAN ONE: I love you too. Or I should say, je t'aime.

Half of a We

I woke up the other morning from a dream. I can't remember the details, but, still sleeping, I said, "I'm so lonely."

In the dream, I had been looking for a birthday card.

The dream echoed the moment, five years ago, when my older son's birthday fell the week after my husband's funeral, held in Minnesota. I had been frantically trying to finish all the things that needed to be done before I left for the airport.

On my long list of to-dos, I added "Buy a birthday card."

It had always been fun to search for the just-right card to send from my husband and me to each son. Sometimes I'd had to go to three different stores in my Manhattan neighborhood to find the card that fit their separate personalities. I was ridiculously pleased with my good batting average.

On this day, with phone calls to be made, my remarks at the reception following the service to be written, flowers to be ordered, clothes to be packed, and more, I knew I wouldn't have the luxury of time to tramp from store to store.

In the closest store, under "Son," there were cards for kids and for adults. It was spring so there were flowery cards. At the back of the stack was one with a pattern of golden leaves.

With a pang of sadness, I opened it to read the message, "Happy Birthday to Our Son!"

I bought it.

Janet and I Talk About Death

BARBARA: Death is such a big part of our day. When you signed up to come here, did you think that would be the case?

JANET: No. I just considered it as a new chapter of my life. A natural progression.

BARBARA: Me too. I was relieved that I wouldn't have to struggle to buy groceries, cook, take out the garbage. But now that I'm here, I feel death walks the halls and follows us right into the dining room.

JANET: I don't understand.

BARBARA: Right now, in this room, there are ten people who are a hundred or more. When I see a spouse, or a daughter or son, I know right away how the very ill person is doing that day. Sometimes the condition flips to a good side, then all look happy and relieved. When the very thin, not necessarily anorexic, eat very little if anything, the servers urge them to eat more.

JANET: I struggle with my husband all the time because he has no appetite.

BARBARA: You do a great job. Because of all the caring people, dying seems to take a lot longer here.

Everything Changes

And just like that, our community changed. A woman who everyone loved passed away, and then another woman did also. And on a separate night, two women died in the space of three hours. Then, over three days, we lost three more residents! In losing our friends, we also lost contact with their children and grandchildren, who'd brought so much fun. Then Dr. Bob went into isolation and Alan moved away after his wife died.

We all mourned. Laughter also died. Residents started dining out to avoid the dreadful silence. Around that same time, COVID swept through the staff and our families, meaning that many of the regular faces were in quarantine, which put an additional pall over daily life here.

But then, surprise! Before we knew it, seven new residents moved in. Five were women, and of the seven, all were intelligent and had lived productive lives. Three of them continued to work even as they struggled to adjust to their new living quarters.

One woman lost her husband only two days after she moved in. In shock, she stayed in her apartment for three days. When she did appear in the dining room, she had no appetite. When the staff brought out her meal, she'd say, "Take it back to the kitchen. It'll just sit here and be a waste." The staff learned to sit her at a table with empathetic residents. She'd listen and sometimes smile at their stories.

There was also a man who'd lost his wife only days before his son checked him in. He moved in a day before his ninety-fourth birthday. He'd been a very successful businessman and an avid golfer and tennis player. He dressed as though he were still at his country club. He, too, had no appetite for nourishing food, only for sweets. But he tells great stories and soon he found companions to dine with.

Another woman's daughters checked her in because her neighbors had either moved away or died. Increasingly lonely, she had begun to sleep around the clock. Here, she's happy and making new friends.

With all of these arrivals, the older residents struggled to learn and remember names—which was even harder because several of the new names repeated some of ours. To add to the name confusion, three new waitstaff members arrived around the same.

I was struggling to learn the name of a new resident who had moved here with his wife. One night I called him Bill; the next time I called him John. Finally he said, "Our names are very easy to remember. We're the two M&Ms, Mike and Monica." Since then, I haven't missed it once.

Tribute to Bob

I delivered this speech when our dear friend Dr. Bob Maddox left the facility to live closer to family.

Dear Bob,

When I arrived here, I was very sick and couldn't eat. My oldest brother had died only days before, and I wasn't sleeping well and having dreams where my brother needed my help but I was unable to do so.

Bob, you stopped by my table to (what I would learn is your standard procedure) to welcome me, a newcomer.

When I told you about my brother, you said I should appreciate his life and all that he had given me, and take his positive traits and use them in my daily life. So at night I'd remember his generosity and his humor, drifting off to sleep at the memory of his low chuckle.

As every Christian holy day approached, I'd become sad and wasn't truly able to enjoy the season.

I was raised in a devout Roman Catholic household where we always confessed our sins every Saturday and received Communion on Sunday. But I no longer believed the tenets, and felt as though I was dishonoring my parents.

At one of your Interfaith Discussion Conversations you explained that we could appreciate and be grateful for our family's traditions without believing all that they had believed.

I did that, and once more I could enjoy the solemnity and beauty of "Silent Night" at Christmas and "Christ the Lord is Risen Today" at Easter.

And during any season, when I get discouraged or sad, I remember the verve and energy that you put into singing "Oh Danny Boy" during the performance of our play.

Acknowledgments

To my biological family: Peter, Laura, Theo, Steve, and Katee; to my Brightview Woodmont family; and to my editor, Britt Peterson, who took my words and turned them into a book, with love and appreciation. Thanks also to Brooke Warner and Megan Milton of She Writes Press, who carried this book across the finish line.

About the Author

BARBARA HOFFBECK SCOBLIC found her lifelong themes in rural South Dakota, where she grew up on a small farm, the youngest of seven children. From earliest childhood, she was alert to the beauties and vagaries of the natural world; she also, however, grappled with a growing impatience to see what was beyond the farm. As a young woman, her drive to break free took her first to serve as a Peace Corps volunteer in Thailand, then travels throughout Asia, the Middle East, and Greece. Back in the States, she described her experiences in a series for the *Minneapolis Star Tribune*. Her first memoir, *Lost Without the River*, was published by She Writes Press many years later, in 2019. A longtime resident of Manhattan, Scoblic now lives in a senior independent living facility in Bethesda, Maryland.

Author photo © Nina Suhin Photography

Looking for your next great read?

We can help!

Visit www.shewritespress.com/next-read
or scan the QR code below for a list
of our recommended titles.

She Writes Press is an award-winning
independent publishing company founded to
serve women writers everywhere.